146
176

Not Servants, Not Machines

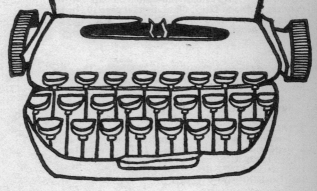

NOT SERVANTS, NOT MACHINES

Office Workers Speak Out!

Jean Tepperman

BEACON PRESS : BOSTON

Copyright © 1976 by Jean Tepperman

Beacon Press books are published under the auspices
of the Unitarian Universalist Association

Published simultaneously in hardcover and paperback editions

All rights reserved

Printed in the United States of America

(hardcover) 9 8 7 6 5 4 3 2 1

(paperback) 9 8 7 6 5 4 3 2 1

We are grateful to the following persons and organizations
for allowing us to reprint material and illustrations:
Questions on the back panel of the jacket and paperback
cover appear by courtesy of Margie Albert; illustration on
page 28 by Francis H. Brummer for *UAW Ammunition* appears by
courtesy of UAW; illustration on page 82 by courtesy of
Community Press Features; illustration on page 147 by
courtesy of Gloria Daily; illustration on page 107 by courtesy
of Geraldine Murphy; and illustration on page 24 by courtesy
of *off our backs*.

Library of Congress Cataloging in Publication Data

Main entry under title:
Not servants, not machines.
    Bibliography: p.
    1. Women — Employment — United States.
2. Discrimination in employment — United States.
3. Trade-unions — Clerks — United States.   4. Women
in trade-unions — United States.   I. Tepperman, Jean.
HD6073.M392U55   331.4'0973   75-36046
ISBN 0–8070–0872–9
ISBN 0–8070–0873–7 (pbk.)

For office workers everywhere, especially those who are questioning, organizing, and demanding their rights on the job

CONTENTS

ACKNOWLEDGMENTS

This book is a product of the office workers' movement. The idea of writing it originally came from Charlotte Cecil Raymond of Beacon Press, who contacted "9 to 5," the Boston Women Office Workers' Organization. The "9 to 5" staff worked closely with me on the entire project — especially Ellen Cassedy, Karen Nussbaum, and Janet Selcer, who helped arrange interviews, read the manuscript and made many useful suggestions, and helped shape the whole book.

Most of the book consists of interviews with office workers and organizers in various parts of the country. Their ideas and spirit created this book, and those whose interviews were not included due to space limitations contributed no less than those workers whose words are transcribed here. In addition, the chapter on the economics and structure of office work depends to a great extent on the analyses of two people: Harry Braverman, in *Labor and Monopoly Capital,* and Margery Davies, in her article "A Woman's Place Is at the Typewriter."

The help of several organizers was crucial in arranging interviews and helping me understand the movement in cities other than Boston: Margie Albert, of the Distributive Workers, District 65 in New York; Joyce Maupin of Union WAGE in San Francisco; Jackie Ruff of Women Employed in Chicago; and Nina Adams and Sue Bucknell in New Haven.

Charlotte Cooper, "9 to 5" co-chairperson, did a great deal of the work of transcribing taped interviews, and helped me edit and interpret them. Mimi McCarthy, Gail

Forten, Rene Martin, and Peg Terry also helped with the massive job of transcribing tapes.

Finally, I want to thank my mother, for breaking ground for me; Gunilla Jainchill, for her help; and Henry Norr, who provided so much encouragement, support, and editorial advice, and made many sacrifices so this book could be written — not just for me, but because he believes the office workers movement is important.

INTRODUCTION

In offices all over the country, two important trends are coming together: workers questioning their treatment on the job, and women rebelling against their treatment as second-class citizens in every aspect of life. Moved by these two currents, office workers are starting to organize, protest, and demand more from their employers.

The new activism among office workers has a special importance both because of their sheer numbers (office workers are 18 percent of the American workforce) and because office work so dominates the working lives of women (one third of all working women are clerical workers). A movement to challenge the job conditions of office workers therefore could make significant changes in American working life.

Why has this new office workers' movement come about? It is the product of several changes:

First, office work has changed. Offices have grown larger, more impersonal, automated. Many offices have started to seem like assembly-line factories, requiring dull and repetitive work, without the chance of advancement that white-collar work traditionally promised. Office work has lost many of its old advantages in pay and job security, which were supposed to make organizing unnecessary.

And women have changed. They are working outside the home for more years of their lives, assuming financial responsibility for themselves and their families. They no longer see their jobs as temporary. With these new responsibilities has come a new sense of independence and of the importance of their work. Yet they are still paid "pin money" and treated like "girls." Working women have been challenging this treatment with a determination that reflects their growing sense of strength.

Recent economic pressures, along with a general questioning of work roles and hierarchies, have contributed to a new upsurge of protest and organization among office workers. But most of this movement's inspiration and spirit seems to come from women who feel a new indignation about their traditional low status, together with a new feeling of identification and friendship with each other.

Eighty percent of all clerical workers are women, most of them concentrated in the lower levels of clerical occupations. As their anger at their treatment begins to produce action on the job, they are joined by many men who share their oppressive conditions and low pay. Still, women's consciousness is the main spark for much of the recent office organizing. This book reflects that fact, by concentrating almost exclusively on the experiences of women. This concentration is not intended to slight the importance of the contributions men are making to the office workers' movement.

More than anything else, this book seeks to provide a forum through which office workers can speak — about their feelings, their ideas, and the movement. Through taped interviews, participants tell about their experiences on the job and in organizing. (In order to protect the identity of many of the people speaking, they are identified by first-name pseudonym only. Most office workers were afraid of having their employers find out that they had given these interviews. This fear reflects the repressive atmosphere and lack of job security in most clerical jobs. In addition, a few of the interviews have been edited for clarity and, in some instances, employers' names have been deleted.) The book also includes a discussion of the economics and structure of office work, to provide a framework for the interviews, and a special discussion about the responses of employers to office worker organizing.

All of us who contributed to the book hope that these stories will give readers a sense of what office work is like, from problems with bosses to the pride of accomplishment.

We hope especially that these stories will speak to other office workers — and encourage them to continue and expand their efforts to join together and stand up for themselves on the job.

Not Servants, Not Machines

1
Old Stories,
New Awareness

How do office workers see themselves and their jobs? How do they feel about their conditions of work; management and supervisors; and office work in general? What are the reasons behind their growing activism?

The office workers movement grows out of many people's personal experiences with employers, jobs, schools, families, and attitudes toward women in general and office workers in particular. Stories shared by office workers provide insight into the reasons behind their growing activism:

LEGAL SECRETARY

Lillian is a young woman who has been a legal secretary for eight years. She is now active in a Chicago group called the Legal Secretaries' Council.

I always thought I would be a secretary. I thought it was all I could hope to attain. Since I was going to be married and have babies, it wasn't necessary to go to college, so I could always work as a secretary until I met a man. I took a business course in high school, typing and short-hand. In high school they told us how much money we were going to make, and I was very much looking forward to making all that money — until I got out and found out it wasn't there.

I became a legal secretary because I thought it would be an interesting field, and I thought they made more than other secretaries. I *do* like the work. I can learn. I read everything that I type. And they do get paid slightly more, but I don't think it's enough. An experienced legal secretary does a lot of work and has a lot of responsibility. But if you compare her salary to what the attorneys make — for instance, I'm making one-sixth the salary of some of the attorneys! I *know* my job is important. And I *know* they can't operate the office without me. I think it's totally unfair economics.

What does a legal secretary do?

If she's allowed to take on as much responsibility as she can, she can draft wills, real estate documents, closing statements. It's not very hard to do this kind of work, really, because there's always something just like it that's been done before. If the clients really knew what goes on in law firms, they would be outraged at the prices. You follow a pattern. It's just like sewing a dress — until you get to corporation mergers and stuff like that. That's where legal expertise comes in. But in my last job I was reduced to being a typist.

Was that why you didn't like it?

That, and attorneys' failing to recognize any personal dignity in secretaries. Secretaries are viewed totally as machines. They are ignored. For instance, if an attorney brings a client into his office, he will introduce everybody but the secretary. Unless he wants coffee, he won't speak to her.

I was talking to one woman yesterday and she told me

that when one lawyer interviewed her, he asked her to get up and walk across the room, so he could inspect her legs. They'll ask you what kind of birth control you use and if it's effective so you won't get pregnant and quit. They want you to promise that you're going to work for them indefinitely. And yet if they decide that you're not working out, they won't bother to talk to you about it. They'll call you in at five minutes to five on a Friday afternoon and say, "You're finished." It's happened to many people I know, for very unjustified reasons, very personal reasons — like he's tired of you. Sometimes they won't give reasons. They'll just say, "You're not working out." Another thing they do is ask you to stay overtime at five minutes to five. When you say you have something else to do, they act like, "Well! How dare you have a life outside this office?"

They moved into new offices in a new building and completely planned everything — didn't even consult the secretaries about typewriters or desks or anything. They just assumed they knew more about the office than the secretaries, and, as a result, they muffed up their whole office.

There was an attorney I used to work for — I used to call him "Mister Steiner." He was only about three years older than me. He was a good attorney, but he was a dimwit. I got fed up with being called "little Lillian," so one day I said, "Oh, Bill, I have a question for you." He stopped dead in his tracks and turned around and said, "What did you call me?"

In many firms, there's a definite atmosphere that says there is an attorney's place and a secretary's place and you better know your place if you want to have a job in that firm. They feel they have gone through many years of school and they know everything about everything, and no little secretary is going to come in and tell them differently. If you happen to catch a mistake of theirs, you can sometimes get hell for that. You're not supposed to read it, you're just supposed to type it. Maybe they have some kind of problem themselves and have to feel like they can dominate somebody. Since they can't dominate their wives, they try with secretaries.

UNIVERSITY SECRETARY

Claudia, Sarah, and Diane are all secretaries at a large Eastern university, all in their twenties, all active in a clerical employees' organization on campus.

Claudia: In the majority of offices, you're stereotyped — an inferior person, not educated — even though you have a lot of skills. Secretaries are very skilled people.

Sarah: They have this idea that you're a servant, that you do nothing but sit around all day long and talk with the girls and answer the phone. Even if you *are* answering the phone, it can be pressure work. You're doing a *job*. You get tired, you get frenzied, you have important responsibilities. If you're answering the phone or if you're typing or if you're an executive secretary or whatever, you have skills; you're an intelligent person and you should be treated as such.

Claudia: So many people have said, "Check with [Claudia] 'cause she'll know what to do." And I do! I'm not being very modest, but I know what's going on around here. And if I know what's going on and if I can run this place while nobody's around, why can't I be rewarded salary-wise? The reason I stay here is because the people I work with are really nice — the bosses, everybody! But I've been here for six years and I make a grand total of $6,200 a year.

Sarah: There are women who have worked here for twenty years, who started out making $2,000 a year and now are making $5,000. I mean, that's pathetic! Clerical, I think, starts at about $4,600 or $4,800 a year for a grade twenty-two, which is probably two dollars an hour. I'm a grade twenty-six. I'm making about $112 a week. A lot of the grade twenty-two's on $4,800 a year are supporting themselves, and how you can support yourself on that sum is beyond me — let alone a woman with a child, and there are a lot of those, too.

Diane: And in this society you're rated on that — how much money you make.

Claudia: A lot of women are impressed with the fact

that they work for a university. You know, they think
that working for "educated people" is just the ritz. "I do
Doctor So-and-so's work and that makes me fantastic."
If people are really impressed with the fact that they
work for a biggie, the university will take off on that and
won't give them raises.

Sarah: And we're consistently left out of everything.
The dean of [the chapel] sends around a letter each year,
inviting people to go to the "light the Christmas tree and
sing carols" thing. He always addresses the letter: "Faculty
and Students." Last year I wrote him back and said,
"You know, there are a thousand staff members. I'm sure
we would like to come to the Christmas tree lighting,
too."

Claudia: There's a mailing list that's used on the campus that goes to "deans, directors, and department heads,"
when in actuality *we're* doing the work that those memos
are talking about. If you've got a good boss, he'll pass
these things on to you, but half the time secretaries don't
even see it.

Sarah: Where I work, we're in a transition stage. We're
disassociating with one department and going over to
another. Whenever there are meetings about budgets, my
boss always has to come to me and get the information,
and go talk to the other biggie who gets *his* information
from *his* secretary — instead of getting the two *secretaries* together (who know what they're talking about),
and getting it done.

My husband — this morning we were talking about
divvying up household duties. He always brings up to
me, well, when am I going to go out and get a decent job?
Because he can't stand what I'm making here. He said
something about how much more important his job was
because he has to go through a five-year apprenticeship.
He doesn't understand why I'm tired at night because all
I do is sit around all day long, use the phone, and all
that. So I was comparing apprenticeship programs in a
trade to more-or-less apprenticeship programs in clerical.
It takes you about five years to evolve into a good office
secretary, department manager, the higher levels of
clerical work. It's the same thing. We work five years,

even seven years, at a ridiculous salary, upgrading our skills.

Claudia: Just being part of an office and learning how to handle people and the way things should be done — that takes time and experience, I think. I don't think I could do what I'm doing today if I were seventeen years old again, like I was when I came here.

TELEPHONE COMPANY SECRETARY

Joanne was happy to be working at the telephone company after bad experiences in other clerical jobs. But a few months after this interview, she was laid off in a general company cutback. Here she talks about the differences in various levels of clerical work.

The higher up you go, supposedly the more sure of yourself you are, the more experienced a secretary you are, the more prestigious, if you want to put it that way, and the more money you get. And you probably work for less people the higher up you go, and you actually do less work.

Now I'm a division-level secretary. All the phone company secretaries are considered management. I work directly for one man. There are six district-level secretaries and if they have a question they come to me. I don't do all the typing for his signature, but before it goes to my boss, it has to go to my desk to be checked over, because my boss won't proofread a letter. He expects it proofread when it comes to him.

In the work that I do, it's not enough to just type and take shorthand. I have to understand. If I see words on paper and they mean nothing to me how do I know if they're correct? When my boss took me, stole me, or whatever, from my other department, he wanted somebody that would have a complete understanding of what he was doing and thinking.

If you work as a secretary, you tend to *dress* better than

you would if you were a clerk. Some of the clerks come in in jeans. If I did that, my boss would probably throw me out the door. I think one of the reasons he hired me was my appearance. It does mean an awful lot. You dress for the job that you have.

I think if you work for twenty people, you don't feel that useful. You're just typing and typing and typing. I'd say that with two or three people, you feel that what you do is important. But then you start getting personality conflicts with your bosses. One says his work is more important than another's. So that can be rough too. I find that working with one person — this is my own personal feeling — you are subject to his moods. People say if you want to know how a certain man is for the day, just look at his secretary!

Do you like working for the phone company?

Yes, I do. I'd have to say they're much more appreciative of the work that I do. I find that they will compliment you on your work. They have a whole system of evaluation for management employees.

Especially now, with the Affirmative Action requirements they have to meet, management is getting used to encouraging women and minorities into higher management positions — by telling them the opportunities that are available, where they can go, what they can do. But of course initiative is still up to the individual. I'd have to go to school at night — I wouldn't get far if I didn't. I would like to be out of secretarial work completely.

How did you get to be a secretary?

I was always geared that way, from my parents right on up. I was told that was what I was going to do, because I never had any ambition to be a teacher or a nurse. And that's what a girl does.

I think it's very wrong that they make people decide what they're going to do when they're fourteen, because you have no idea at that age, the middle of eighth grade. And if you take clerical courses, it can make a lot of difficulty for you later on if you decide to go to college.

If I really had a choice, I wouldn't have taken secretarial
at all. I would have taken something like business
management.

What was your first job?

I worked for [an insurance company]. They said it was
clerk typist. I didn't know I'd be sitting in the typing
pool all day. If you took a college course in high school,
you were given a higher title — clerk typist — and made
more money. But if you took the clerical course, you
were called just a "typist" and put into a typing pool and
made *less* money. I thought that was very strange.

Our department typed the exact same form over and
over and over. Fifty times, a hundred times, four hundred
times. I didn't know what I was doing. It wasn't explained
to me. They just said, "Type it." I wanted to know what
it was.

If you got up from your desk you were told to sit
down. If you looked around, you were told not to talk.
If you went to the ladies' room too many times, they'd
tell you. I was told they counted the papers in the waste-
paper basket. I did work with one woman who used to
rip up the used papers, put them in her pocketbook,
and flush them down the toilet. You were clocked in and
out. You went to work by the bell, you went to break by
the bell, you went to lunch by the bell.

No matter how good you were doing, they'd tell you,
"I think you could do better." I was evaluated, so to speak,
once. You had to fill out worksheets of how much work
you did during the day and account for every minute
of your time. That I didn't like. If there were fifty cards
in a pack and you did five, they'd look at it and say,
"Wow, you only did *that*? You have got to work a little
bit faster now."

Later I worked for a private investment firm. When I
had that job, I was sick for over two months. I had
worked for them eight months. When I came back from
being sick, they fired me. I had a lot of hard feelings
about that. I got some sick pay, but no disability.
You don't get disability unless you are management — all
men. You were a man, you got these benefits. You were

a woman, you got those benefits. I was out of work a total of four months.

That's another thing. The economy and office work go hand in hand. If the economy is tight, secretaries get less pay and have more work piled on them.

INSURANCE SECRETARY

Emily is a middle-aged woman who works in a one-boss, one-secretary branch office of an insurance brokerage firm.

When I was married, I worked as a receptionist off and on. But it wasn't really until after my husband's death that I had to return to the business field.

I worked awfully hard — I was new to insurance, and studied and took courses. I worked on holidays, I worked nights. But after I got into it, I found that the boss I had was incompetent, that he was an alcoholic. He would go out to lunch and have too many martinis. I remember days when I would lock him in his office when there was somebody around who shouldn't see him in that condition. When somebody tried his door, I'd say, "Oh, there's a conference going on." I would protect then, but I won't protect anymore. They don't deserve it. Would they protect a secretary if she did this? No way! She'd be out the door so fast!

I did it then because I was of the old school. I thought,

no matter what the circumstances are, you must always
be subservient. That's the way we were trained. I went
to a secretarial school down south, in 1943. You were
trained in those days that when a man entered the room
and he's a bigger person than you are on the totem pole,
so to speak, you stand up. And you'd be surprised
how hard it was for me to start breaking that habit. They
told us that you never question, that you were there to
do the work and the reason they were in their position
was that they had more knowledge. It's taken a lot of
re-education to change my attitude, but just thank God
it's going, with a lot of other old hats that needed to be
changed!

So I was all gung-ho on insurance. But I have been just
turned off so much now with seeing, for example, cases
of brokers who have had two or three offers from various
companies. Now, you would think that if they had their
client's interests at heart they would naturally sell their
client the policy with the lowest premium. No way.
They sell the one with the *highest* premium, because of the
commission. It means more money in their pocket. There's
very little honesty in it now. This is part of the hang-up
I have, because I really hate being part of something
like that. I have known insurance agents who really are
sincere. But they're few and far between.

And life insurance reinvests into so many different
things. Even into political campaigns. Like Clement Stone,
for instance. He was one of Nixon's biggest contributors.
They just own so much of everything else. They invest
their money and make more money.

What about the job you have now?

Right after I started, my boss was on the phone one
day. Apparently a call hadn't come through and I heard
him say, "Well, I don't understand. I was right here, and
my girl was here too." So I let him finish talking and I
went in and said, "When you refer to me, you may refer
to me as Mrs. Rogers, Emily, my assistant, my secretary.
But don't you *ever* call me your girl." And, stupid that
he was, he said, "I wasn't inferring any romance." I
said, "Don't worry. I wasn't either. But I'm not your

chattel." So needless to say, we don't get along too well.

My boss's expense account for the office is thirty thousand dollars a year. That includes the car, the telephone, the rent and *my salary!* The directive came from the home office that whatever he saves from his expense account, he will pick up as an end-of-the-year bonus! I found this out just before my boss came in and said to me, "I just want you to know that I'm not recommending any salary increase for you. Now or ever." And I said, "May I ask why? Is there something wrong with my work?" And he said, "You know Goddamn well there isn't anything wrong with your work. I just don't like your attitude."

We have a sales-contest period. Certain quotas are established, and during that period if the head man makes his quota, he gets a bonus — and a nice, substantial bonus. So everybody has to break their back during that period. Well, for some reason my boss made his quota last November. And I had to work twice as hard, which I didn't mind. However, he picked up a check for an eight-hundred-dollar bonus in addition to his commissions. I didn't even get a thank you.

I have to send in a time slip twice a month to the home office, showing that I started work at such and such a time, and that I go to lunch for one hour, and when I quit. And I have to submit it to my boss to be signed. Now, he doesn't have to do anything like that. I have a petty-cash fund, and even if I spend twenty-five cents I must get a receipt and attach it to the petty cash slip and send it in. He can spend up to twenty-five dollars without having to show *anything*. It's this whole thing of putting down rules for one class as against another class.

COLLEGE RECORD CLERK

Marge is a mother who went to work at a suburban woman's college when her children reached school age. She works in the Development Fund Office, receiving and

*keeping records of alumnae contributions. Like many office
workers, she feels that her official job grade doesn't match
her actual work.*

Although they have nine grades for personnel, I know
of only one person who has a grade six. Nobody seems to
have a seven through nine. We all seem to be in three
or four, a few in five. Yet if you look up the job descriptions, there are very few of us with those grade three
and four jobs that suit the descriptions. We do a lot more
responsible work, decision-making. They wouldn't call
it decision-making. They'd call it going over their heads.
But when they leave the office, they're only too glad to
have somebody handle their work for them.

We work under tremendous pressure in our office.
Right now we're into the centennial program. We're
trying to raise seventy million dollars. My first question,
when I heard that, was how much of it was going to be
given to staff salaries. There was dead silence.

In order to cope with the centennial drive, they have
increased the number of directors, but they haven't
increased proportionately the number of people who are
working in the office. It's impossible to cover that amount
of detail work and get it done accurately. Consequently,
I'd say, in two months a lot of people are going to write in
and say, "Why wasn't I counted as a donor? Why am I
being asked for another donation?" Proofreading is so
important, putting address changes away is so important —
things I've always considered important because that's how
I was trained. Either you're very conscientious, or you
don't care.

They have staff meetings. I would like to go, and I've
asked, but they say I would have nothing important to say.
What they say is, "If you have anything to say, tell me and
I'll pass it on." A lot of ideas that you might have, to make
work more enjoyable or to shorten the time you have to
spend on a particular project, are picked up by somebody
else, and maybe two months later they're incorporated into
the office procedure. I think the person who thought them
up should get credit for them, at least get a pat on the
back. But that's not the way it works.

Most of the people who work here are in their forties. The college would rather hire somebody in their forties or fifties. If they haven't had jobs before, or if they don't want to go too far from home, they're only too happy to get a job [here], only too willing to take less pay. It's good for [the college] because employees won't be so dissatisfied with their jobs and they'll plug along. They want you to feel [the college] is very maternal. It's a suffocating type of feeling. There's a sickening-sweet atmosphere.

PUBLISHING COMPANY CREDIT ANALYST

Maureen has worked for years in New York publishing companies, in secretarial work and credit offices. At the time of this interview she was planning to move to Texas and leave it all behind.

When I was sixteen, I never thought I would be a secretary. Never! I think I wanted to be an adventuress or something — something you can't really formulate at sixteen. Just something a little special, a little more fun, a little exciting, you know — *freer,* than a nine-to-five. I think I always wanted to be a cowgirl. To be out on the range and hang around and stuff like that. I don't know. But unfortunately you get trapped. It's a sad story, very sad.

I'm not an heiress that's just doing this 'cause it's kicks. I need my income, very definitely, but it's never been the primary thing. I think that's why I changed jobs so often, for the sake of change, because everything becomes so deadly awful and boring and picky.

Did you have problems with supervisors?

My boss at [one company] thought if he went out and had fourteen martinis for lunch he'd really be showing everybody how cool he was. Then he'd come in and just *demand* to know why all these *dollars* weren't collected. There was a vast, vast amount of work to be done by a really small staff. He'd waste all your time bringing you in the office and asking you why these things weren't done, rather than if he took a lesser lunch hour and got down and took on some of these accounts himself.

We all got up in arms about him because he was really outrageous, just demanding absurd things from people. We used to go en masse to personnel. It was absurd to be listening to this man rattle on, drunk as a skunk every day. And then we were told that the next person who went to personnel to complain about this man would be fired on the spot. Now isn't that a marvelous way to handle a personnel department?

And there were so many supervisors, that by the time it got to the top man to say yes or no for me to sharpen my pencil, fifteen, twenty levels would have passed! It's just fantastic! You know, they kid you along as though, yes, you have some kind of responsibility, but you *know* anything you say can be negated by anybody on this string.

I'm a credit analyst right now at [a different house]. The credit department determines who will and who won't get books, making sure that the payments come in regularly. You get on the phone to people, you cry with them, you laugh with them, you turn them over to an attorney, and you try to help them — primarily just to get money in. I do like working with people rather than just a desk and ledgers. But it gets so detailed, so terribly detailed. And I think I'm tired. Five years of it!

BANK TELLER

Janice has now transferred within her bank, from her position as teller to a job as clerk in the department that handles international trade transactions.

Being a teller was my first job, just out of college. I graduated in a year that was really bad, as far as getting jobs — 1971.

How did you feel about working as a teller after going all the way through college?

Crummy! Really crummy. I graduated in liberal arts, majored in Spanish. I felt angry, disgusted about it at first. I guess you sort of get used to it.

Did you enjoy being a teller?

It can go both ways. You meet a lot of people. It's sort of fun to talk to people. You develop your own clientele. You get to know them and sometimes talk to them about their jobs or whatnot. But on the other hand, one nasty person can wreck your whole day.

It was challenging to balance, too. In the afternoon you have to add all the cash you've taken in and subtract all the cash you've given out from your first figure, then count your money and see if that's the same figure. If you were off, trying to find the mistake could be a little bit interesting. When I was assistant to the head teller, I found it was interesting to help other people balance. Just the challenge of trying to figure out where they would have made the mistake.

Why did you leave the teller job?

Boredom. And the customers. They were really getting to me. People being rude. Sometimes in a public-service position, people don't really look at you as a person. You're just like a machine, and when they get a little bit frustrated in what they're trying to do they just *tear* at you! It's not *your* fault, but they'll take it out on you.

When I have a line of people in front of me, I feel like I have to keep working faster and faster until they're gone. It makes you nervous! It can be very pressured. You're working with a lot of money. You've got the responsibility of this person coming up to you. You have to make sure you can cash this particular item. Is it good? Does the person have a balance? Is the signature accurate? Is it made out properly? Did he endorse it properly? Is this type of identification acceptable? It's just endless!

For a while I was a collections teller. As that, you didn't wait on customers. Collections are like when checks go through a clearing house, one bank trades them to the other. There are some items that can't go through the normal procedure and then you have to type up a letter for every single transaction. It's *very* time-consuming. I was also supposed to be a backup teller when it was busy.

But because we were shorthanded, my supervisor was *always* telling me to open my teller window, and I couldn't get my work done. You'd walk away and just get situated with something, and then she'd yell at you to open. Then you would go over and wait on two customers, shut your window, and go back, and it was just this back and forth and back and forth. It would drive me up a wall.

For a teller, the only place you could go is like where I was, doing special things like being the collections teller. So I put in for a transfer, figuring that at least I could go to another department if I couldn't go up. Then a guy was hired in the teller line. He was only supposed to stay six weeks, to learn every operation. Then he was supposed to go upstairs to bookkeeping. He was my age, he had a two-year community college degree, and he had less experience working in a bank than I had.

I watched him — he went from one department to another and spent about a month in each department. Then finally the assistant to the operations supervisor quit and he took over the job. I was really angry about it because I didn't even know there was a position open. This information was just not divulged. I mean, all the time they do this! They'll prefer to hire outside the bank for any position that means anything, rather than to look around inside the bank at these perfectly qualified people. The head teller made some crack about, "You know *he's* going to go someplace because he wears pants."

What do you do in your new job?

Now I process international documents. When they ship something, I have to check all the documents, check the credit, type up the tickets, type up documents. I like the work. It's very interesting. But everything has to be initialed and checked and rechecked. They give you no responsibility whatsoever. *But* at the same time, if its done *wrong,* it's brought right back to you. Even a twenty-five-cent commission ticket, you have to have *initialed* in triplicate or quadruplicate, and then you have to rip them and this ticket goes there and that ticket goes there. It's just insane.

Right now is a particularly slow period in my department. It's been *awful* slow, just *awful!* I have nothing to do all day, but I have to *look* busy. It's miserable. I write letters a lot. Sometimes I clean up my desk.

How would you change the bank if you were in charge?

In the teller line I think they should have them do other things that are a little bit more interesting, like the balancing and the bonds. Usually the collections teller or the note teller will take care of special jobs, but if they spread that out among the girls, it would make it more interesting for them.

In my department they have each person doing a different job. One girl will do all the import business, one will do letters of credit, and so on. I think it would be better if they separated the work by client company instead. That way you'd be doing different things, which is interesting. You *should* learn all of it. And if you're doing the same company, you become familiar with the way they like to settle things, and you'd be calling them up all the time and getting to know them.

I thought if I learned a lot about banking, maybe I could make a career out of it and, you know, *get* someplace. But it just seems like a dead end. I think it's interesting, but you have to fight to find out things! To learn things, you have to keep quizzing people and bugging people. My immediate supervisor seems very sympathetic. He wants to switch the department to have it by company. But he seems to be fighting a losing battle.

TELEPHONE OPERATOR

Chris is a mother in her thirties who has been, in her words, "everything" — factory worker, waitress, supermarket cashier, insurance clerk, and telephone operator. She is

*now enrolled in a community college and hopes to become
a social worker.*

I had a commercial course when I was in high school.
This is what I was geared for. My family didn't have the
means to send me to college. But in my house you didn't
work in factories. You went to school and worked in an
office and considered yourself better than the people in the
factories. When my mother was twelve years old, she was
made to go into a mill. Her family were immigrants from
the old country, and a woman's role was that you were
taken out of school and put in a mill. It crushed my mother
because she had all A's in school. And when she had her
own kids, she wasn't going to have them go to work in a
mill.

But at [the insurance company], it was just like a factory.
They had piecework and everything.

Was the phone company an improvement?

No, because I *can't stand* anybody checking on me. I'm
not a kid and I don't like to be treated like a kid. Each
G.C.O., which means Group Chief Operator, had so many
girls under her charge. They wouldn't tell you when, but
she plugged into you at least five times during the month,
to make sure you were saying "please" and "thank you,"
that you were doing everything the way you should be, at
the proper speed.

What if you did something wrong?

You'd get a demerit. Seriously! A demerit! If you got
enough, they had reason to fire you. Say you said, "Direc-
tory assistance. May I help you please?" and the caller
didn't know the first name. If there was more than a column of names, you were supposed to tell her, "Gee, I'm
sorry. I can't look it up. There are too many." If you went
through that whole thing and forgot to say "thank you" at
the end, you got a demerit! If you gave out the wrong
address, you got a demerit. The calls were only supposed to
take five, six seconds.

You had an average. If your average was one hundred
percent or ninety, you weren't doing too bad. They pre-

ferred it to be ninety-eight to one hundred. When you got
to eighty, forget it! You were in really big trouble. They
would actually harass you, and I mean *harass* you. They'd
bring you to the desk where the G.C.O. was sitting and
say, "This is ridiculous. You're supposed to learn the job
right." And it was little *minute* things — like, if you gave
someone a number, but they had said [one suburb] and it
was really in [another], and you didn't *say* [the right sub-
urb], you got a demerit. You work under a terrific amount
of pressure. They were perfectionists — the phone company.

They really wanted you to be in fear of them. You
couldn't talk back, you couldn't speak out of turn. When
certain G.C.O.'s walked in the room everybody'd go, "Oooo,
shut up! shut up!" It was really like school. If you didn't
conform, you were out. You had to *really* conform to be
able to move up. It didn't mean you would be good in a
managerial position. You were just proving that you
weren't going to challenge them, by doing everything they
wanted. Anybody who challenged them, forget it! They
didn't want to be challenged.

If you did well and you weren't absent for a whole year,
they'd take you out to eat. Isn't that wonderful? And if
you did very well and went three months with no mistakes,
you got a charm. They used to give you a bracelet with
the charm, but that turned out to be too expensive, so they
just gave you the charm. You had to buy the bracelet.

I think people in offices are conditioned to be passive.
Maybe they're divorced or have financial problems at home
so they need the money and put up with a lot. I think
they get awful bitter, awful resentful, but they keep it in.
What can they say? Where can they go? It's either a factory or an office. There are not that many things that a
woman can get into.

And most women have been trained to feel that this is
all you should expect. Isn't it true? We were taught this!
If we have a nice job and we're secure and getting paid —
hey, be grateful! You're a woman. The hell you should
want anything more!

But they're not happy. They show it by picking at each
other. Rather than go bitch at the boss they take it out on

each other. Either "She's getting too much work," or "She's working too fast," or "How come she gets a break?" I think this is why women are catty sometimes. Because they're not allowed to be themselves, or to be free, and they resent it deep down. They really resent it. Because everyone likes to feel that they have something to contribute.

TELEPHONE COMPANY ACCOUNTING CLERK

Celia is a payroll clerk and Debbie works in the billing department for the phone company. They both work indirectly with computers, preparing information and checking errors. Debbie is also union steward (representative) in her office.

Celia: I love my job, really. It's an interesting position. And I enjoy it because, in the background, I'm working with people — people at my own level, so to speak. Most of them are workers. I don't have too many managers.

I used to work as an operator, twenty-odd years ago, when I first got out of school. At that time it was a very very rigid thing, but I enjoyed it. Then I got married and had to leave. At that time it was a rule. The chief operator explained to me that usually when you get married, you end up having family problems. I won't use her words because I can't remember, but I understood it to mean that you should be like a machine, so that you have no problems and no sickness. I mean, you just show up every day because they push a button.

Debbie: Now they have a system of giving people "contacts" when they've been out sick. It means you're spoken to. It seems that if you've been out three times you get an oral contact, four times you get a written, and the fifth time you get a final. And if you're unfortunate enough to get sick after that they can suspend you, or they may not pay you for some of the days that you've been out sick.

Celia: You know you have a job to do and that you're supposed to be there at eight o'clock. Now, if for unforeseen reasons you're *not* there, and you fulfill your obligations — you do phone in — but then you get spoken to, that hurts. Because you're giving all of yourself, as much as possible, to do your job, and yet they're not appreciating it. It takes a little bit out of you. You think, why am I doing it? Why not just sit back and be another little nail in the wall?

Debbie: Even girls who have been pretty good kids as clerks — once they become supervisors, they change.

Celia: I think they get into positions that *they* have someone to answer to, and I think they forget to be human beings; they become part of the establishment. Perhaps they're told, "The workers are the workers and you are the boss, and you keep the workers in their place and you stay in your place." And I think that after a while they feel as though they are the king. They begin to believe it.

Debbie: Besides, their raises are based on appraisals and their appraisals are based on the work produced out of their units.

If you could change your office in any way you wanted . . .

Debbie: Get rid of management!

Celia: We'll run the business for a while!

Debbie: I think when you sit there as a clerk, you see a lot of things that they do backwards. You would maybe use a more logical approach. I think I'd like to see more flexibility. And I think I'd do away with job levels and just make everybody equal.

COUNTY HOSPITAL BILLING CLERK

Nancy's job is to prepare patient information for the billing department. Partly because of her confrontations with management over sick leave, she has become active in her union.

I had a problem with sick leave. I had gallbladder trouble and I would have terrible pains at night and the next day I would have no evidence of ever having had any pain, but I had been up all night suffering. So at times I was only out for one day. I was nineteen when it started, and twenty-one before they realized what it was. I suffered for two years like that. At work they wanted me to bring in a doctor's notice every time I was off ill. I resented it a little, but I went along with it because I knew that I did have a sick-leave problem. But then my supervisor said she not only wanted the doctor's excuse, but she wanted the doctor's diagnosis, and I told her that was none of her business. That led to the personnel manager. He suggested that maybe I should take off from work and wait till my health was better. And they did try to dock me one time. It was a whole big hassle.

I had twenty-three days off in one year and we're allowed twenty-two. I had had surgery that year. My coworker, who happens to be white and older, had nineteen days off and didn't even have surgery. They never asked her what it was and they never doubted her at all about her sick leave. They questioned me, I think, because I was young; the fact that I was black was secondary. But I think there *are* a lot of racist supervisors. They'll watch a black person more, and be a little harder.

In my office, the first two blacks were hired in November of 1972, a week apart. They did not have one black worker in that office before then. They may have a certain percentage that are black now, but they're not in any high positions. They'll stick one up there, a token black and that's all it is. I think that they have the ability, I really do, because I believe that when you're black, you can't afford to be good — you've got to be great. But there are a lot of others who *also* have that ability who don't get the chance.

INSURANCE COMPANY TYPIST

Linda is one of a growing number of clerical workers with computer-related jobs. Her work and the exactness with which it is checked are typical in computerized operations.

I use a typewriter. It types numbers on different forms and sends information to the computer banks in [the home office]. It really doesn't take much brains. Mostly manual dexterity. The forms are self-explanatory.

Everything is time-rated. On a particular time-rate you're supposed to be able to put out x number of pieces of paper a day. You have to keep track of it. Each sheet has a number that automatically goes on the tape when you push the button. So you can't really cheat.

The actual work involved doesn't bother me. It's really not exciting by any means. It's not even that interesting. But it's not that boring. It just doesn't *go* anywhere. The people who sit next to me have been there five, six years. There's no way they're going to go anywhere. I don't want to sit there and type. I think I'm smarter than that. The biggest promotion is, if you're lucky, they might make you a secretary. That's the top of the totem pole.

One thing we were just talking about at work is noise pollution. It's very loud. And the machines are not easy to type on. It's like — especially for a machine that was designed to be typed on all day long — driving a big truck with standard, without automatic steering. It's very hard and it's very noisy. I can't hear anything when people talk to me. Everybody there thinks their hearing is impaired. A couple of years ago my supervisor mentioned it to management. They said, "Well, we'll investigate it."

And the petty regulations. You have to ask permission to leave the floor to get a box of cigarettes. You have to ask permission to do just about everything that involves leaving your desk. And then there's late slips. I can see late slips. They're documentation of your attendance. But not for a *minute!* I think there should be reasonable leeway. Five

minutes is the difference between walking up the street fast
and walking up the street slow when it's icy. Or missing
the bus. But people get slips for being late by a minute. It's
incredible. I can be very conservative when it comes to
rules. I believe in rules, as long as they're reasonable. But
things like that completely undermine your dignity.

I think everybody gets tired of doing what they're doing.
I think if they got paid adequately, or even if they thought
what they were doing was important, they wouldn't mind
doing it. Actually, if you look at the whole scope of
clerical workers, what they're doing is more or less the
heartbeat of how the business is run. And the managers are
getting paid to organize and manage these people. And
then they kind of look down on them, when in fact it's the
clericals who create the managers' jobs. I'm sure we
could do without all the managers. But if we went on
strike for a day, then nothing really would happen!

They look at us as "just" typists. I don't think anybody
likes to think of themselves as that. That's why I don't
want to do it forever.

They're telling us that they're changing things, that
they're having all these meetings. They think they know
all our problems and that they're going to help everybody
out. But they don't have the meetings with the *employees*.
They say it's none of our business! I would say that very
few men in that company have any conception of what
it's like to sit and type all day, or to ask permission to
go to the bathroom.

The attitude they have now is just, "We've got you over

a barrel because you need the job." The morale is very, very low. Everybody feels it. Management doesn't care. They quite blatantly don't care. I've seen the manager or the assistant manager go over and kick somebody's desk because she had her head down, resting or something. It just lets you know the attitude is, "Hey, we're paying you — you keep working."

CHECK-SORTING MACHINE OPERATOR

Nora works on the evening shift in a large bank. She operates a computerized machine that "reads" magnetic ink code numbers at the bottom of checks and sorts them into pockets by bank branch.

In our area we have about sixty or seventy people, about ten women. Before, they had no women working because it was a man's job — working with a machine. They didn't think women could do it. If it breaks down and it's nothing really big, we fix it ourselves. They show us how to fix the wiring and a lot of things, because it costs the bank money when you have to get IBM to come over and fix your machine. I like to work with my hands. It's kind of nice to work with mechanical things and not let the machine run you.

A lot of checks are not supposed to go through — like certain checks that should go to another bank or forged ones or some that the number isn't quite clear enough on. Unfortunately, once in a while some of them will slip through. Then you have to ring the buzzer and they have to come over and rebatch everything. And they know that sorter such-and-such let them go through. Now they have error sheets, so every time you make an error it gets marked down. People are making more errors now because they're so nervous about not making them.

It's for performance reviews. They want statistics when

it comes time for raises or promotions. They started marking down errors in January, but they didn't let us know until almost the end of the month. All of a sudden they hand you an error sheet. We didn't think it was fair not to let you know. It's almost like Big Brother.

A new thing that came out, too, is down-time. They have a log sheet, and you have to mark down every time your machine is not running. If you go to talk to somebody, you write down, "From 7:10 to 7:20, talking." Or you have to mark down when you go to the bathroom.

These performance reviews, down-time, things like that — people are very upset about them. You're working faster because "items per hour" is going to be part of the statistics in your review. At the beginning of the night, there's very limited work because the branches haven't all got in yet. So people are almost fighting to get work, because they want their item count up there.

You have to stand on your feet constantly. When you're feeding the machine, you're moving to empty the pockets at the same time and turning around to fill up the tray and putting the tray when it's full to the other side. I got used to it. You just keep going.

They don't have any fresh air circulating and you're breathing in dust all the time with sixty people and thirty or forty machines going. There's a lot of dirt because the checks give off a lot of dust.

But the conditions aren't too bad, as far as working there. I enjoy going to work. The work isn't hard. Our whole group gets along. When we have breaks, and even during work, we have a good time joking with everybody. We have good talks.

Most of the people agree with me that they don't give you enough training on what happens to the check. They'll say, "You're running D.D.A. today." Fine. I know that D.D.A. means you're running the main type of work with the orange separator card, but I don't know what "D.D.A." means. It means debit something. Or "D.V.," or "S.D.A.," or "G.L.E." — you know, all these words. It would be nice if you knew what they were or where the checks come from or where they're going. It's just a feeling of not knowing. It's like the machine running you. You're like a computer. "We'll run D.D.A. today."

COMPUTER DEPARTMENT AUDITOR

Ellen works for an insurance company, proofreading "jobs" before they are sent to the computers. Any error that goes through costs the company expensive computer time. "Maybe they haven't had a mistake for six months from you," she says, "but when one does come through, they're on your back."

I like the work itself. I want to be a computer operator. But the time they were going to move some people into operations, I was told it would be people that they thought were "prepared." But then they took trainees off the street — people who had no contact with this kind of work before at all. I mean, Willy Lump Lump. We had, I think, one woman who was an operator.

To be an insurance broker, a woman will have to have a B.A. And let's say she's got six years of experience. Here comes some guy, straight out of high school, maybe a year or two of college. They tell her, "Well, Mrs. X, you train Willy here." She trains Willy, but when there's a management position open, Willy gets it.

In my department there's a girl — she's been there seven years, longer than anybody else. One guy came to our department. She trained him, and after she trained him (they're doing the same work, she's been there longer) his job grade was higher and his pay was higher and he's the guy that's supposed to be the supervisor now.

If you see a guy, you know his grade is thirty-six or over. And most managers are men. You can always tell who's who, just by their sex.

Are people also discriminated against because of race?

Yes. Well, it's not something that's said, or else it's said in a joking manner. But you can tell it's there. Like my boss, for instance — he'll say little snide things, and if you turn around and go, "I beg your pardon," he laughs it off. "Oh, I was just joking." That type of thing.

Did you plan to be a clerical worker in high school?

No, I *did not!* I was going to school. I wanted to teach nursing. But I ran out of money, so I decided I'd stop and get a job. And at that time it was about the only thing I could get.

The pay is lousy. I started at $490 a month. I'd been there for six months and you know how big a raise I got? Fifteen dollars more a *month!* When it showed up on my paycheck it was like seven dollars more. They told you that you would get your raise by the amount of work you did and how well you did your job, but you didn't! They have a budget. When they're talking to the supervisor they go, "Well, the price is $550, but when you go to interview this person, see if you can get 'em for as low as you dare go." And that's the way the raises are. Give them as little as you can and then if they pitch a bitch,

Francis H. Brummer for *UAW Ammunition*

"Don't think of it as a decrease in salary. Think of it as a shot in the arm for the company."

you tell them, "Well, you'll have to talk to the boss" — which a lot of people will not do.

And they were telling me about all these programs that I could take to better myself. *But* the only thing they ever give is typing courses! Or something clerical.

Plus you do not get paid for maternity leave. One girl worked up to the last week of her pregnancy, and she wanted to know if she could use her sick days, because she had enough to tide her over. She could not! Well, there's one guy who's overweight. I mean he's really overweight. And he kept pulling the veins in his legs. I think he took two months off. They wrote this down as a disability and he got paid.

They like it if you dress nice, but in most of the departments you can't afford to dress nice because you end up tearing your hose, you get dust on your clothes. And it gets very dusty in there.

But OK, you wear jeans, an old pair of pants and blouse. They look at you funny and tell you, "We can't have you representing us and meeting the public appearing like that." But you only meet the people that work there!

ACCOUNTING-DEPARTMENT UNIT LEADER

Judy worked for four years in the accounting department of an insurance company. Her work was to use an adding machine in figuring out agents' monthly bills and commissions. After this interview was recorded, she quit that job to work full time organizing office workers.

Now I'm the unit leader. It doesn't really mean much except that you relay messages from the supervisor to the rest of the people who work in the department. She gets her instructions from the home office. Nothing creative anywhere along the line. I have seven people that work with me, and I'm supposed to be responsible to see that all their work gets done.

When they're late, they're supposed to give me a reason, but I never ask, because I don't think it's any of my business. I'm supposed to report the excuses to somebody,

but I don't. Some of the other unit leaders go up to
somebody and tell them to stop talking and get back to
work. But I can't see how anybody could work for seven
hours straight without stopping to talk! We've been told
that we have to watch when the girls go to the bathroom.
I told them I wouldn't do it!

They say the employees have a right to complain. It
just isn't true. They'll listen if they want to. But if they
don't think you're right, forget it! There's no impartial
judge. If I have a complaint with my supervisor, who do
I go to? I'm supposed to go to my supervisor. If I go
higher, they say, "We'll talk about it." And then they go
back and tell the supervisor exactly what I said. And
then she's mad at me.

Two friends of mine were almost fired because they
were talking about their salaries. You're not supposed to
tell each other how much you make, and this girl who had
worked there for a year and a half found out she was
making five dollars less than somebody who had just
started. She had a fairly responsible position, and she was
very angry. She told our supervisor, and the supervisor told
the manager and the manager called them both in and
said, "We *would* fire you, but we like you. So don't let
this ever happen again."

I think there's a lot of competition among the unit
leaders — to be the most powerful, I guess. It's kind of
absurd. I think the company encourages it. They tend to
give out meaningless titles like assistant to the assistant
to the assistant. I think that tends to encourage people to
think they have a lot more power than they have.

I was yelled at one day a couple of weeks ago for
changing my lunch hour. I told everybody, but my supervisor said to me, "Don't you know that you're supposed
to ask *permission* to change your lunch hour?" And then
on our afternoon break, this woman who works with me
said, "I'm going down to the first floor to buy a card."
And the supervisor, who was the same age as this woman,
said, "Are you asking me, or telling me?" It was *rude*.
It was a mean thing to say — just to show her power.
It seems to me like she thinks she's in a powerful position,

and she's not, really. Because she just relays messages
from higher up.

All unit leaders and supervisors have to go to meetings,
usually once a week. Most of the time it's to tell us stuff.
The only kind of input we get to do is in very small
procedures. They pretend to consult us a little bit, but it
ends up that we have to do it their way anyway. I think
we spent three days talking about our Christmas party.
Those kinds of things can go on forever and ever.

I'd really like to do something that meant something to
me, rather than just make money for an insurance company. I don't think [the company] cares anything at all
about its employees. They just don't have any respect
for the work we do. They think that any idiot can do it.
A lot of our work is very technical and time-consuming
and it has to be very very exact. I think that's the thing
I hate most. They just don't think we're important at all
— we're *just* clericals.

BOND MANAGER

Bev is one of the few women who have been able to
work their way up in insurance companies, from typist to a
more responsible position. But there were hassles every
inch of the way.

With three years of college behind me, they told me
that this job held the promise of becoming an underwriter
in the near future. So I sat every day and typed up insurance binders. They were a form, they weren't even something you had to think about. After six months of that
I got fed up and walked in to my boss and said, "Really,
I come in in the morning and I turn my mind off. I
really don't feel that I'm being utilized, and I thought I was
going to learn more." "Well, Bev, you haven't been here
long enough." So after another six months, *still* nothing
happened. They kept telling me I didn't know enough

about insurance, and I said, "That's because no one's *teaching* me anything about insurance." I used to read the policies, just to see if I could pick up something. Then finally in the bond department, two people were leaving jobs as bond clerks. When I tried to get the job, they kept saying, "We'd like to hire someone with experience." So, for one of the jobs, they hired a girl with four years of college and a degree in sociology. Finally, after much harassment, they said to me, "OK, if you think you can do it."

After we had been working in the bond department about a year, our boss quit. He had to give a month's notice, and it was another month after he left before we finally got fed up and said, "Hey, what are you going to do? Are we going to come in Monday morning and find some man sitting there saying, 'Hi, I'm your new boss'?" We were *doing* all the work. So they said, "Oh. Well, gee, we don't know. Boy! Can *you* do the job?" We said, "What do you mean, can we do the job? We *do* the job!" And they said, "Oh. Well, gee, we'll let you know." So after another two weeks they brought us in and said, "Well, you really think you can do this, girls?" And we said, "Yeah, we really do." So they said, "OK, you two are co-bond-managers!" And they gave us a twenty dollar raise apiece. He was getting $300, and now we're getting $150 each. So we're getting half his pay, doing his job, *plus* our old job. And they think we think, "Oh, great!"

I happen to really like my work. There's something different every day. I do have that so-called managerial responsibility, and I really enjoy it. It's a lot of fun. I just wish I could get the respect and have people realize that I *do* know my job — instead of their constantly waiting for us to flounder so they can say, "Ah ha! You *can't* do it!"

There was no such thing — I don't think there is yet — as a woman bond underwriter in this city. People still call and say, "May I please speak with so-and-so," and we say, "Well, he's no longer here. May we help you?" and they say, "Then can I speak to the bond man who *is* there?" And we say, "I'm sorry, *we* are the bond man here." "Well, who is your boss?" "Well, we are our bosses." "OK, well, *maybe* you can help me." And every time that we can't get something rushed they say, "Well, gee, looks like you don't pull much weight in the companies." And of course we're still sitting at our desks *outside* the office, which is empty now!

In this firm the men wear the suits and ties and sit in the offices, and the women get their coffee, get their sandwiches, fix their bouillon. A lot of women say they don't mind doing it, but at the same time they *hate* doing it. It's tradition. They're afraid to go in and say, "I'm sorry, I don't want to do it anymore." Men will even get up, walk to the women standing at the coffee wagon, dump a dime in their hand, and say, "Can I have a regular?" I mean they're *right there!* We're told to "Xerox this for me" or "would you get me a pack of cigarettes downstairs."

They ask you (no matter what your degree is), "Can you type? Here's a typing test. You're a woman — take it." My boss, before he left, asked for a typewriter, and they told him that they do not allow the men to have typewriters, because "it just doesn't look good. I mean, could you just see someone coming in and seeing a *typewriter* at your desk?"

In January, 1973, when I first started working here, they linked onto a worldwide insurance brokerage firm. That's when the changes came — like people being laid off. They got rid of a lot of older women who (*they* said) didn't have enough to do. I think they started with women who would be collecting pensions soon. They did let a few men go, but they gave them notice and severance pay, because the men are all under contract. Five o'clock on a Friday afternoon they brought in women and said, "You don't have to come back Monday." I'm not kidding.

The paranoia in that place for two months was incredible. They knew they had you right where they wanted you. Women are afraid now to tell you anything about their jobs because they're so afraid that if you learn their jobs, maybe the company will let them go and let you do their work. It's constantly over your head.

ASSOCIATE EDITOR

Lois and Elaine both work in editorial departments of publishing companies. Lois is in her late twenties; Elaine, a middle-aged divorced mother. As college graduates doing editorial work, they are considered professionals. But they have faced many problems similar to those of clerical workers and they, like many other publishing employees, are beginning to organize.

Lois: When I first started, I did secretarial work. The other half of my job was working for the editor-in-chief, reading manuscripts, writing jacket copy, that kind of thing. I have a friend who graduated from college at the same time I did and who also did some graduate work, and when *he* went into publishing, he was made an associate editor the minute he walked in the door. Nobody asked him to be a secretary. We had exactly the same qualifications.

I've been in publishing for eight years, and I think that I was held back. Maybe I'm wrong, but I have a feeling that when men come into publishing, they are really pushed ahead, whereas women have to grab for everything.

I feel that women have for a long time been grossly underpaid and underutilized. This is a glamour industry. For a long time there were a lot of women coming out of colleges with good educations but no particular skills. Well, they thought it was very nice if they could rub elbows with the great, so to speak, and be in an intellectual surrounding. For a long time we just overlooked the fact that we were being paid *nothing* to do this work.

I think the reason there is organizing going on now is because women have finally said to themselves that they are not going to take it. They are not going to be satisfied with doing someone else's work and not getting the credit. I think inflation had something to do with it, too. And women are beginning to have a sense that they don't want to be dependent on their parents or a husband any more. They want to have a career. They want people to take them seriously and they find that maybe they are *not* being

taken seriously. So I think all of these things are coming
together at the same time.

Elaine: Management is all men. Right down from there,
it's solid women. Women come in as secretary or typist.
After secretary it goes editorial assistant, assistant editor,
associate editor, editor.

Salaries are really bad, work pressure, responsibility that
is forced without any sort of compensatory salary or
advancement — the whole *company* will *close* if you
don't have this deadline met. And while it's exaggerated,
it is the sort of business that does have deadlines. There
are real reasons why there are pressures, but there's never
any compensation. There's a lot of overtime work, but
in the history of the company they've *never* paid time-
and-a-half. People have worked sometimes eighty hours
a week, week after week, and gotten just what the
company chose to give them — compensatory time off a
year from then, or the following summer.

The company is forever sending memos saying, "We
work from nine to five. We don't work from nine-fifteen
to quarter of five." And "We don't want you to just pick
lunch and go whenever you feel like it. You either pick
a twelve o'clock lunch or a one o'clock lunch." There's
really no reason for this. People don't pay much attention
to it, but they also sort of resent it.

The longer people stay, I think, the more bitter they get.
Imagine a woman who's worked fifteen years, who's a
full editor, who really knows her job, who's devoted an
awful lot of time and energy. On a textbook, we write a
lot of the material ourselves. We write stories, we write
the teachers' guides. You really think up the ideas and
plan. So this woman has put in fifteen years of her
life. Suddenly she realizes that her salary doesn't compare
with some man of her age and experience.

I like editorial work, I like the responsibility. But I
want to get paid for the responsibility.

TEMPORARY SECRETARY

*Laurie worked as a temporary secretary for four and a
half years off and on. During that time her feelings about
being a temp changed a lot.*

At first I was very apologetic about doing it. It was
really upsetting my family — the whole thing that you're
basically unreliable, that you won't commit yourself to
anything. To myself I said, "Well, I'm just looking for
something really good."

I worked for [one agency] for about fifteen months —
all this time trying to look for something that had some
substance to it. Being in and out of offices and seeing what
jobs are really like, you wouldn't take them in a million
years. You also know how scarce jobs with any *meat* to
them are. Unless you want to spend fifty years typing at
one desk, most of the jobs are bad.

The advantage of working "temporary" was that I didn't
have to put up with any S–H–I–T from anybody. I remember one guy who hassled me to death. He told me
where every period should go, how many spaces there
should be on the page — all this garbage. He was just
unbelievable to the woman who was the permanent
secretary. She got ninety-nine percent of the flak and I
got what was left over. After about three days I called
the agency and said, "Please replace me." So they did.
I only did that two or three times in four or five years.

After a while of being a temp, I changed my attitude.
I got tired of being apologetic. I took the attitude,
"Look, if you don't approve of it, that's your problem. This
is the way I choose to work." Business stinks for women.
As a temp, you meet new people, and at least the scenery
changes once in a while.

Although I'm sure that in most people's eyes I was
wasting time, I *was* gaining experience, skills, and making
judgments about industries and companies. I enjoy
responsibility. I had a lot of it even when I was working
temporary. They let you take the responsibility, but they

won't give you the recognition or the credit or the money for it.

As a temp, you start taking pride in the fact that you are very adaptable, that you can get along with people, that you have those kinds of skills. A lot of people can't work that way. They can't adjust. I liked that aspect of it. I think I learned a lot. I became a very good secretary.

On the other hand, when you work temporary, there are no benefits, no insurance coverage. If you're off sick, if you can't get work, you're not paid. It can get pretty rough. And the pay at [the agency] was pretty bad. After all that time, the top I was making was $3.35 an hour. And I was one of their top people.

Temporary work is a big business. [The agency that I worked for] has two hundred offices. The bigger they are, the less money they pay you and the larger the agency fee is. [This agency] made something like two or three million dollars profit last year. They're crying and moaning about the economy, and they can't give women insurance, and they can't do this and they can't do that. I don't buy it.

When you were a kid, what did you think you were going to be when you grew up?

Never a secretary. Never. I think I wanted to be an artist. I've rationalized that — I still draw, I still paint. There are some things in business I like, but I refuse to be just another bolt in the machine. I don't have to set the world on fire, but a job has to be personally satisfying.

2

Office Work:

Some Common Myths

The idea of office workers organizing or protesting seems strange to many people. It conflicts with so many of America's stereotypes of office workers, and women in general. It also seems strange because of common assumptions that office work is both privileged and unimportant. The growing movement of office workers challenges these myths, and makes it important to look at the truth behind them.

1. OFFICE WORK ISN'T REALLY IMPORTANT
(*or* YOUR JOB DOESN'T DESERVE MORE MONEY)

A hundred years ago, as American corporations grew larger and more complex, a boss could no longer personally do all the work involved in running a company. Bookkeeping, correspondence, billing, inventory, became huge operations in themselves. The demand for clerical workers grew along with the economy: in 1870 they were fewer than 1 percent of the workforce; in 1900 they were 3 percent; by 1970 they were almost 18 percent of the workforce — nearly one in every five workers.[1]

As the country grew richer it demanded more services, more banks and insurance, more government work. Big companies grew into monopolies, credit buying replaced cash, and the tentacles of American business spread out over the world. All these developments added to the economy's dependence on clerical work. In the words of a sociologist in the early fifties, "Each office within the skyscraper is a segment of the enormous file, a part of the symbol factory that produces the billion slips of paper that gear modern society into its daily shape." [2] Now the paper has been partly replaced by punched cards and electrical impulses. But clerical work is still the nerve system of corporate society.

In the "office industries" (banking and insurance), clerical workers are about half the total workforce. In public administration they are well over a third, and in transportation and utilities, a quarter. In service and wholesale trade, clericals are about one fifth of the workforce, and they are over ten percent in manufacturing and retail trade.[3] In all, there are about fourteen million clerical workers in America.[4]

In a society that judges a person's importance by her paycheck, clerical workers rank low. But imagine what would happen if all the clerical workers got fed up one day and stayed home. Finance, insurance, telephone, law, and government offices would grind to a halt. Manufacturing companies would be thrown into chaos. Phones would be ringing. Irate customers would be demanding services no one could perform. Nobody could communicate or get paid or be billed. Orders couldn't be sent out or be filled. Nobody would know where anything was. The importance of "unimportant" office work would suddenly become clear.

2. A SECRETARY IS (AND SHOULD BE) AN "OFFICE WIFE"

The job of secretary, like many other women's roles, has been studied, debated, glorified, and condemned. Traditionalists praise secretaries for being supportive, efficient "helpers." Secretaries' training programs and advice books emphasize tact, smoothing out conflicts, creating a pleasing environment — office homemaking. The books are full of checklists for "telephone usage" and "office personality." Most items on these lists deal with the secretary's manner, such as "displayed interest" and "injected polite expressions." Secretaries are warned against "going beyond their decision-making power." They are taught procedures for "How to Do Your Employer's Personal Work Effectively," including travel arrangements and Christmas gift lists.

Secretaries are coached in using their secondary, dependent position to their own advantage. The author of *The Working Girl in a Man's World* explains how to rise in the company by helping your boss succeed. "Your fortunes are bound up with his," she says. "If he's going places, so will you." [5]

But the role of secretary as "office wife" is now being questioned by secretaries themselves, by their organizations, and by their employers. Secretaries are saying they don't want to be defined, ranked, and paid according to the man they work for. They want to be judged and rewarded on the basis of their own efforts and skills. They object to duties that have no purpose but to make the boss seem, and feel, important — the ritual of making coffee, the ritual of the telephone call. "When my boss wants to make a call," one secretary said, "he stands there holding the phone while I dial, then we both stand around waiting for the other person to come on the line. It's ridiculous."

The National Secretaries Association is an organization which tries to overcome the image of secretary-as-servant by projecting an image of secretary-as-professional. The organization encourages secretaries to feel a justifiable pride in their skills, knowledge, and experience. It even offers the degree of Certified Professional Secretary to people who demonstrate enough experience and pass an exam. But this program touches only a tiny percentage of office workers. Even if the NSA achieves its goal of doubling the number of CPS's by 1980, this group will still be only one half of one percent of the three million people classified as "secretaries and stenographers," who in turn make up fewer than one quarter of America's fourteen million clerical workers.

An equally serious limitation of this approach is that employers can just ignore it. The NSA can point to a few companies that give small bonuses to people who pass the CPS exam, but most organizations classify secretaries, along with other clerical workers, as nonprofessional. They are definitely not given professionals' benefits, pay, or status.

Meanwhile, management experts are also doing some rethinking about the role of secretary. Many argue that it's inefficient for anybody but the very top executives to have private secretaries. Most bosses, they say, don't generate enough work to keep a private secretary busy. A secretary then becomes primarily a status symbol — and companies don't want to pay extra salaries just so their junior executives can feel important!

Many of the things that can make a secretary's job enjoyable are regarded as inefficient by these experts. In secretarial schools women are trained to establish their own procedures and organize their offices. But experts advise companies to standardize and routinize, to apply uniform systems and procedures in every department. They leave less and less room for initiative, even on the part of lower-level executives, not to mention secretaries.

For all these reasons, most secretarial work is now done by secretaries who work for more than one boss — sometimes two or three, sometimes up to twenty. The bigger typing jobs are handled by typists, either in the department or in a typing pool. The secretary's work is divided up as much as possible into different specialties. More and more people do the same operation all day long.

As clerical work becomes increasingly routinized and specialized, offices become more like factories for processing information. Many clericals work in huge rooms, with rows of people sitting at desks or machines. Even if they sit in small offices that don't *look* like factories, the work is often organized on an assembly-line basis, with each person doing only one step in the whole process. The close work relationship of the private secretary to her boss has grown less common, as huge, impersonal office organizations have developed. One file clerk at John Hancock said, "My manager has only talked to me twice in five years — once when we were stuck in an elevator together."

---

3. OFFICE WORK IS A STEPPING-STONE INTO MANAGEMENT

Traditionally, white-collar workers are supposed to be loyal to the company because they work closely with management and hope to become part of it someday. Companies encourage this hope, while, in reality, there are many barriers to moving up. Any woman can tell you one: "You have to be ten times better than a man to get anywhere." "They'd *never* put a woman in *that* job." Most women can usually hope only for promotions from the typing pool to a secretarial job, or to supervisor of the typing pool.

But even male clericals find, as one union staffer put it, that without a college education, you can only "bump the floor of middle management." [6] As educational qualifications get more rigid, "working your way up" becomes more of a myth. A few men may jump over this barrier in some fields. Women hardly ever can.

Most companies are organized in a way that makes promotion difficult. A clerical worker in a large modern office rarely has the chance to get to know people in management. And typing information on forms all day probably doesn't prepare her for any other job. Besides, most higher-level employees are recruited from outside the firm — usually college-educated white males. Few companies regularly post job openings, and many require employees to make transfer requests through their supervisors, which effectively discourages job-hunting.

But the most important reason that promotion into management is mainly a myth is that there aren't very many management jobs. In the words of an MIT administrator, "upward mobility is limited by the pyramidal structure." [7] A vice president of the First National Bank of Boston went even further. "You know how the bank is set up?" he said. "Like this," and he traced this shape in the air:

"Where can they go?" he asked rhetorically. [8]

Sex, age, race, and educational discrimination largely determine *who* will join the elite few. And with the way companies are set up now, it's still only a few.

---

4. MANAGEMENT TAKES GOOD CARE OF ITS WHITE-COLLAR WORKERS

At the turn of the century, office work made up only a small part of the budget for most companies. Bosses could afford to be generous with salaries and fringe benefits, to win the loyalty of the small white-collar staff.

But with the growth in clerical work, office salaries became a major expense, and cost-conscious managers started eyeing the clerical payroll. One executive wrote that the secretarial-services department should be considered a "profit center, just like sales and manufacturing." [9] An office management textbook states, "In most organizations there can be little doubt that the office area constitutes the greatest frontier for economy." [10]

A hundred years ago, when clerical workers were few in number, and mostly men, the typical clerical worker earned about twice as much as a blue-collar worker. [11]

Now the average clerical income is *less* than the average production-worker income.[12] It is also well below the Labor Department's estimate of the income it takes to keep a family of four at an "intermediate" standard of living.[13]

Now, with more clerical workers, it's important to companies to save on each clerical salary. Also, most office workers have not protected themselves by organizing unions, as blue-collar workers have done. Another reason for the relative decline in clerical pay is the fact that most office workers are now women, and employers are accustomed to using women as a source of cheap labor.

One government study that showed the average pay of clerical workers to be lower than that of production workers then broke down the figures by sex. *Male* clerical workers make more (though not much more) than *male* production workers. *Female* clericals make a little more than *female* factory workers. Both categories of men made more than both categories of women.[14] This makes it quite obvious that it is precisely because most clerical workers are women that the average clerical pay is lower.

There is no reason to think companies are being especially generous to office workers because they are "white collar." On the contrary, employers of white-collar workers make special efforts to avoid paying more than they have to for clerical work. In Boston, for example, major clerical employers have formed the Boston Survey Group. Through this organization they periodically report to each other on how much they're paying the "girls" these days. They also get together for quarterly meetings to compare notes on personnel policies.[15] The information they exchange can be used to keep clerical salaries uniformly low. If you know all your colleagues are starting file clerks at $90 a week, it's pretty easy to figure out that you don't have to offer $100 to get a file clerk.

Businessmen's organizations also lobby in state legislatures against bills that might force them to be more generous with employees. Manufacturers' associations, bank associations, and the film industry lobbied in the California legislature against a bill to preserve and extend the rights of women workers.[16] In California, as in many states, some benefits (like rest breaks) were required only for women workers, under old-fashioned "protective" laws. In the last few years employers have been eliminating these benefits, claiming that they were discriminatory. Their lobbyists turned out in force against a bill that would have protected these benefits for both sexes.

The Associated Industries of Massachusetts, another business lobby, led a campaign in that state against a bill that would have forced companies to give accrued sick pay to employees out on pregnancy leave.[17]

On the national level, the Chamber of Commerce has testified against pro-labor bills, like the ones that would protect the rights of public employees to organize.[18] And insurance executives from Mutual of Omaha, Combined Insurance, and Continental Insurance, among others, are big contributors to lobbying efforts against the Equal Rights Amendment.[19] This amendment would force insurance companies to stop discriminating against women, not only as employees, but also as customers.

In all of these businessmen's organizations and lobbying efforts, employers of office workers are active participants. "White-collar" status is no protection against the efforts of employers to keep their labor costs down.

5. OFFICE WORK IS BEING UPGRADED AS MACHINES ELIMINATE ROUTINE, LOW-PAID JOBS

The use of office machinery began with the typewriter, in the 1870's. By the 1920's, calculating, billing, addressing, and duplicating machines were transforming clerical work. The big changes in the past twenty years have been photocopying and offset printing, new developments in typewriters, and, especially, the boom in the use of computers. Private companies started using computers in the early fifties. By 1970 there were 63,000 computers in use or on order,[20] and almost all banks and insurance companies used computers in their operations.[21] The computerization of office work is still taking place, with more companies buying computers, and computers taking over more and more jobs.

In typing, the main new development has been the typewriter with a memory. This "word-processing machine" stores form letters on magnetic tape or cards, and types them out automatically at 160 or 180 words per minute, stopping for the typist to insert names or special information. This means that "individually typed" form letters can be produced many times faster than before.

Some people see in these developments a hope that office jobs will become more interesting, as machines take over more routine work. But the fact is that the file clerks whose jobs are eliminated by computers rarely get hired for higher-level computer-related positions. They are the wrong sex. Studies of office computerization show that companies usually bring in higher-level computer personnel from outside — usually men. In a typical insurance company data-processing center, 93 percent of the lower-level jobs are held by women, while only 15 percent of programmers and analysts are women.[22] Men with only high school degrees are often hired for these positions, while a woman usually has to have a college degree to become a programmer. And even programmers, while they make somewhat more than typists, are not lavishly paid. Much of their work, too, has become routine through advances in computer technology.[23]

Most of the jobs automation creates are routine and low-paid, such as keypunch operator. There are many more keypunch operators than computer programmers. And automation makes other jobs *more* routine. Information must be standardized so the computer can process it. Because computer time is so expensive, office workers must meet tighter deadlines and more exact standards of accuracy.

The word-processing machine is sold with claims that it "frees the secretary" from routine work. But it *can* do just the opposite. A typical machine sells for about $8,000, so it, too, must be kept in operation. Therefore many companies assign secretaries to operate the word-processing machine all day. One former secretary who now trains people to operate word-processing machines said, "All we

do is chain the secretary to a machine. We only freed one
secretary and that was me."

---

6. OFFICE WORKERS ARE SAFE
FROM LAYOFFS

Because office work has become such a big expense,
companies are less likely to keep people around the office
if they don't need them. Like high pay, office-job security
used to be real — about 75 years ago. Layoffs and firings
were then less common in the office than in the plant.

But in recent times of economic trouble, companies have
laid off office workers as well as plant workers. In the auto
industry crisis of 1974, for example, many thousands of
white-collar workers were laid off by auto manufacturers.
Economic problems have encouraged companies to stream-
line office operations. Chrysler estimated that it could cut
2,500 of 5,000 jobs by consolidating clerical operations in
two of its Detroit plants.[24] Similar reductions can occur
when a big firm buys up little ones.

Automation has also led many companies to reduce their
office staffs. One executive estimated that 6.5 secretaries
with magnetic-card typewriters could do the work of 22.5
secretaries with regular typewriters.[25] Studies of computerization have shown that computers often reduce the need
for clerical workers — by 133 people in one insurance
company,[26] by 328 people in one bank.[27] When automatic
dialing systems are introduced, many phone company offices close, or reduce their workforce drastically.[28]

Machinery enables each employee to produce more. In
times of economic expansion, companies can use this increased productivity to get more work done. But during
recessions or depressions, companies can be expected to
use "labor-saving" machinery to save them the salaries of
some of their office staff. Some companies reduce their office staff by simply not hiring anyone when an employee
quits, and thereby avoid layoffs. Some others just tell
people not to come back Monday. Because so few office

workers are unionized, most have no protection against whatever the employer decides to do.

None of this means, however, as some people claim, that machines are making clerical workers obsolete. Many jobs can't be done by machines, and even when they can, people are needed to operate the machines. Hardly a computer in the country "knows" anything unless a person — usually a low-paid woman worker — tells it the information on a keyboard. In the most advanced computer systems, keypunched cards are no longer used. "The girl just keys in the information directly," said one bank officer. The "girl" is still an essential part of their multi-million dollar computer system — even if one of the cheapest parts!

---

7. YOU CAN'T GET HURT ON THE JOB IN AN OFFICE

Every day many blue-collar workers risk violent accidents, even death. Offices, as workplaces, are relatively safe, but accidents and injuries frequently do occur. People often trip over wires and electrical plugs in the floor, and sometimes break legs or sprain ankles. Poorly arranged offices can be real obstacle courses, and make moving around difficult, even dangerous.

A major health problem in big offices is noise pollution. A room full of operating machines can cause real emotional and physical harm, including loss of hearing. Inadequate lighting, or glare, can cause headaches or eyestrain. Typing all day is famous for causing backaches, especially if the company hasn't bothered to provide well-designed chairs. Certainly sitting all day is a health hazard in itself — why shouldn't companies provide exercise facilities?

The air in offices may contain substances dangerous to inhale, such as fiberglass particles from central air conditioning ducts, or fumes from correction fluid. Electronic stencil machines give off ozone gas, which can cause throat irritation, coughing, drowsiness, and headaches.

And the work itself can make you sick. Work under time pressure, to keep up with production quotas or deadlines; work that "drives you crazy" because it's so boring; bosses and company rules that show disrespect for you — all these things produce stress. Many office workers keep tranquilizers and aspirin in their desks to get through the day, or take frequent sick days. This stress can add up to real physical problems — headaches, high blood pressure, ulcers. Women are taught to feel that problems like these are imaginary, or their own fault. But they are real health problems, and jobs often create or contribute to them.

---

8. WITH ALL THESE NEW FEDERAL REGULATIONS, BEING BLACK HELPS YOU GET A GOOD JOB

In clerical work, as in most aspects of American life, talk about equal opportunity covers up a pattern of persistent racism. Racism is documented in statistical studies. For example, a 1972 report on banking found "a statistical pattern of employment discrimination against minorities and women," a "massive and intransigent refusal" by banks to cooperate with the study, and a failure of federal agencies to enforce the law.[29]

Racism is also clearly visible to anyone who walks through a big office company. Pretty, young, white women work as private secretaries, in the carpeted offices of the new downtown buildings. Black clericals are mainly reserved for the keypunch room, the typing pool, or the data-processing center across town — the routine, pressurized, low-paid jobs.

Historically, clerical work has been a privilege of dominant ethnic groups. At a time when most workers were from recent immigrant families, most clerical workers had native-born parents.[30] Black people and other minority racial groups started entering clerical work in large numbers only in the mid-sixties, into the jobs at the bottom of the clerical range, especially keypunching. Blacks still have less chance than whites of becoming clerical workers — fewer than one-quarter of black women workers were clericals in 1973, while more than one-third of white women workers were clericals.[31]

---

9. WOMEN CAN BE FOUND IN EVERY JOB THESE DAYS

Today many previously all-male occupations include a few women. But a recent Labor Department study found that most women are still concentrated in the same industries and occupations they have been in for decades. Caroline Bird has invented a term for the concentration of most women workers into a narrow range of occupations: "job ghetto." Since it's still hard for women to enter most fields, many women are forced to take clerical and service jobs. Because employers know that women have few alternatives, they can pay low salaries and still feel confident that many women will have to take these jobs. In spite of recent changes, there are still huge female job ghettoes. And clerical work is the biggest. *One out of every three working women is a clerical worker!* That's one reason why a movement to organize office workers is so important.

When clerks were a small elite, they were usually men. As soon as offices started needing clerical workers in large numbers, they started hiring more women. By 1900 about one-quarter of clerical workers were women.[32] By 1970, over three-quarters of all clerical workers were women. It is the only major occupational group in which women outnumber men.

Why were women chosen for clerical work when it started expanding? First, and most important, it was because they were cheaper to hire than men. It was also safe for a male executive to teach a woman secretary all about his work, since there was no chance she could compete

with him later on. Women were thought of as docile and obedient, with manual dexterity and patience for detail work.[33] (Even a few years ago, an office workers' newsletter quoted a boss describing a clerical job: "I don't think a man would be appropriate for this job. He'd quickly get bored with the work." [34]) And men just liked having women around to cheer the place up, take care of their little personal wants (things it would be harder to ask a man to do), and lend a touch of home to the office.

But mostly it was because women were cheaper. And as we will see, this is still true.

Within office occupations, women are concentrated at the lowest levels. (This is *not* because they have less education. The median number of years of education for all clerical workers is 12.5. The figure is the same for black women, white women, black men, and white men.) In *banking*, to quote from the 1972 report on that industry, women are concentrated in "low-level, tedious, poorly paid jobs, and the outlook for advancement is bleak." [36] In *insurance*, to use Boston as an example, women hold 86 percent of clerical and office jobs, while men hold 88 percent of managerial, professional, and sales jobs.[36] In the *federal government* itself, over three-quarters of women are in the lowest six grade levels, but fewer than half the men are.[37] Only 3 percent of women, but nearly one-quarter of men, are over grade 12.[38]

There may be a few women in every job. But most women still work in the job ghetto, with paychecks that show it.

---

10. WOMEN ARE CATCHING UP TO MEN IN EARNINGS

In America today, among all full-time workers, the average earnings of women are less than 60 percent of the average earnings of men.[39] This is a *decrease* from 1950, when women's average wage was a little over 65 percent of men's.[40]

In clerical work specifically, there is also an increasing pay gap between women and men. In 1962 women clerical workers were paid an average of 68 percent of men's pay — by 1971 it was down to 62 percent.[41] This is not only because women are concentrated in the lowest-level jobs, but also because women are paid less than men *within* job categories. In insurance and banking, for example, according to studies done in the sixties, women were paid less than men in every single job category in both industries, even when the jobs were classified by experience and grade level.[42] For example, bank tellers with five years of experience earned more, on the average, if they were men. More recent information, such as a 1971 study of the Boston insurance industry, reveals the same pattern.[43]

---

11. GIRLS WILL WORK A FEW YEARS AND THEN GET MARRIED

In 1900 the image of the office worker as young and single was accurate. At that time, two-thirds of secretaries and typists were under 24 — four-fifths were single and living at home.[44] Employers used these facts to justify low pay and lack of opportunity. Though this old justification is still used today, by 1960 the median age of women clerical workers had already risen to 35, and over half of women clerical workers were married.[45]

This is part of a general change in women's working lives. The average woman now works for 25 years — 43 if she's single.[46] Fewer working women leave their jobs to get married; the majority of them are already married. Fewer quit to have children, and those who do return to work sooner. Now almost 30 percent of mothers with children under three are working. Over half the mothers of school-age children work.[47]

Women are an important and permanent part of the labor force, and work outside the home is playing a more important part in women's lives. This is one reason why more women are challenging the second-class worker status they have held for so long.

12. WOMEN DON'T DESERVE TO EARN AS MUCH AS MEN BECAUSE THEY ARE ONLY WORKING FOR PIN MONEY

Two trends are making women's earnings even more crucial to themselves and their families: changes in family patterns, and the rise in the cost of living. Many women stay single, and many are divorced. These women must support themselves, and often children too. Many more are married to men who are unemployed, or earn very low incomes. The Women's Bureau estimates that at least half of all women workers work because of "pressing economic need."[48]

Women are not working for pin money. But even if this myth were true, employers are not usually so careful to take a family's needs into account when they decide how much to pay a person. Maybe they should. It would be

nice if companies volunteered to pay people more if they
had a lot of children or a sick spouse. But until they do,
why should they feel justified in paying women less because they supposedly "need" their incomes less?

---

13. OFFICES HAVE TO BE SET UP A
CERTAIN WAY FOR EFFICIENCY

It's fashionable now to write about the problem of alien-
ating, boring work. Clerical workers haven't received much
of this attention, maybe because they are women. But much
clerical work involves routinized, repetitious activity, and
many office workers feel that the work itself is their major
job problem.

Because we are so used to the way workplaces are organized and jobs divided, it's hard to imagine that it could be
different. But any organization starts with a big task to do,
and then *decides* how to divide that task into jobs for particular people. Almost all organizations in this country follow the same basic pattern. But this pattern is not the only
one possible.

Managements are pushing more and more "specialization" — making sure that the person who sends out orders
isn't also receiving invoices, making sure that the typist is
never interrupted by a person asking a question. The main
principle of modern office (and factory) organization is
to break down work into the simplest possible jobs, then
hire people to "specialize" in only one of these jobs. Managers claim this is the most "efficient" way to run things.

Efficiency just means reaching a particular goal with as
little "cost" as possible. Costs can include money, time, effort, pain or unpleasantness, and effect on the environment.
But, traditionally, companies have considered only the
money costs. In most American organizations, the goals are
to produce the highest possible profit, and to keep top management on top. Work is organized to further these goals
while spending as little money as possible. This is how the
American economy defines efficiency. A company could be

very efficient by this definition, but very inefficient if it is evaluated with other goals in mind (like producing high-quality products, or the personal growth of employees), or if other costs are considered.

Breaking most of the work down into repetitious, routine jobs has some obvious disadvantages. People get bored and tired. Some get angry, others lost in space. Morale tends to be low, which also hurts the company, since people take too much time off or get careless. One management argument is that "specialization" is efficient anyway, because a person gets very good at a job she does all the time. This argument is mainly phony. Most routine jobs can be learned in a very short time. Once you learn the job, you don't get better at it by doing it year after year.

Another phony argument is that if people do the same thing all day, they won't waste time switching from one task to another. This might be a reason why an employee should do one operation for an hour or so. It's no reason why she should do the same operation for *years*.

One of the *real* reasons why jobs are so divided up is that it gives management more control over the whole organization, and the chance to make more of a profit (or save money, if it's a nonprofit organization).[49] If each worker is doing only one task, the supervisor can control the work more completely. It's easy to *measure* how much work people are doing, and set standards to force them to work faster.

Sophisticated methods for doing this have been developed into a business approach called "scientific management."[50] Not all offices measure work, but experts now estimate that over three-quarters of all clerical work *could* be measured and given production standards. A full-fledged application of scientific management would have three parts: defining exactly *what* the person should do, stating exactly *how long* it should take, and then using these standards to force people to work faster.

In the first step, job analysts figure out exactly which motions are the most efficient. For example, one management text shows a chart for analyzing the motions used to type a form. There's one column for each hand. Every motion is a separate step — reaching for blank paper, grasping blank paper, moving it to the typewriter, inserting it, etc. In this example, the typist was shown to be inefficient because her left hand was idle while her right hand was setting up the work. The company was paying that left hand, but it was sitting around doing nothing! The solution was to tell the typist to get blank paper with one hand while she was getting the handwritten original with the other, saving valuable seconds of the company's time.

Whether or not companies go to this extreme, they can go on to the next step: setting time values for each job. This form should take 2.6 minutes to type; these cards should be punched at the rate of 30 per minute. Then employees can be required to keep track of how much they really do — or the machines they use can be set to keep track automatically.

When the company knows exactly how a person measures up to its production standards, it can use this information to decide whether to give her a raise or a promotion, reprimand or fire her. Some companies give keypunchers and typists "production bonuses" — extra money for doing more than the quota. This may sound fair, but it's just an office version of piecework, which factory workers have fought against for years. They have seen that in practice the rates are low and that the system is used to goad people into working faster and faster for the company. The purpose of all of this "scientific management," from the company's point of view, is to increase profits by getting more work out of each person.

"Specialization" also means that very few workers understand the entire picture of the company's work. This is great for the managers, because it makes *them* important. They're the only people who know what's going on. If the employees knew how to run the place themselves, they might insist more on being listened to.

The philosophy behind modern management is that a few people at the top should have as much control as possible over how the work is done. In addition to job analysis, management texts have whole chapters on how bosses can keep control of filing systems. They are told to issue manuals with rules about what and how to file; to make "routing charts" for incoming mail, giving deadlines in minutes for each operation to be performed. One book, in discussing the problem of photocopy-machine abuse, suggests that the office manager "periodically examine discarded copies left by users."

Of course, most offices don't live up to the ideal of total control of the work process from the top. But many live up to it closely enough that office workers are forced to follow detailed procedures they may not understand or agree with.

Is it "efficient" to have a few people plan the work for everybody? Isn't it possible that people involved in doing the work would be able to make decisions about it at least as well? Some companies, like Volvo in Sweden, give work to teams instead of individuals, and let the teams decide how to get the work done. This approach has been used in a few offices in the United States. But most companies reject this idea. Management wants to make sure that the company is run to *its* liking. After all, workers might decide that improved working conditions or better customer service were more important goals than stockholders' profits.

Perhaps the main reason for dividing most work into routine jobs is that it's easy to justify paying low wages for these jobs. This plan — having most of the work done by low-paid workers — is another principle of modern management. It is frequently mentioned in arguments about whether the secretary should get the boss's coffee. As one secretary explained, "They say that since the men get paid more, their time is worth more to the company. Makes you feel great! So therefore you are wasting less of the company's money by going to get his coffee so he can continue working." If low-paid workers do all the work *they* can do, it "frees" managers and professionals to do the important, creative work that only *they* can do. This sounds so logical that it's important to stop and analyze it.

The company definitely does spend more money on a manager's time — say $10 an hour — than it spends on a secretary's time — say $3 an hour. So his time *is* worth more. But it's a vicious circle. It's the *company* that de-

cides to pay that secretary only $3. Then the company uses this as a reason why she should do all the routine work.

But it's not just salary, management would argue. A manager gets paid more because he has more knowledge and ability. At the same time, everyone knows that knowledge and ability are at best only part of the reason why Mr. Big is a $10-an-hour executive and Janie is a $3-an-hour secretary. Some other reasons are that Mr. Big is white, male, and a college graduate. Being white and male doesn't mean he has any abilities worth $10 an hour. Being a college graduate may not either. Most organizations automatically look for a degree when filling positions over a certain level. But the fact that Mr. Big studied eighteenth-century English literature doesn't necessarily mean he knows more about the company than Janie, who has been working there for years.

However, Mr. Big probably knows more about his job than Linda, who works in the typing pool. The question is, why? It's because he is involved with many aspects of the work and has a chance to learn about the whole process, while she types information on forms all day. But that, too, is the company's decision. If they defined her job differently and gave her a chance to learn, her time would become "valuable" too. Of course, they still wouldn't want to increase her pay, since they're trying to keep down costs.

This is exactly what happens with many secretaries.

They *do* know their bosses' jobs, and even do their bosses' work many times. But they're still paid a "clerical" salary. This leads to problems of discontent and requests for raises. So it's better for the company if most people are uninformed and limited in understanding. This may make them more willing to accept their low pay gracefully, since their jobs aren't "worth" any more.

But what is Mr. Big really doing with his valuable, $10-an-hour time while Janie is getting his coffee? Maybe he's working. Or maybe he's standing around waiting for the coffee, or arranging a golf game. Maybe he actually spends more time getting her to do the work than he would spend doing it himself. One office workers' newsletter describes what one boss did when he wanted a calendar removed from his door. He wrote a memo telling his secretary to remove the calendar. Then he walked down the hall to his secretary's office and gave her the memo. Then he returned to his office. Meanwhile she also walked down the hall to his door, where she removed the calendar, and returned to her office.[51] In textbooks and on organizational charts it looks sensible to save Mr. Big's time for work that only he can do. But in real offices, most higher-level employees don't work all the time. That's one of the benefits of being higher up.

Because of this, many companies now try to do away with private secretaries, forcing executives to get their own coffee and make their own phone calls. But the same argument applies to other office tasks. Why can't managers spend some time at the keypunch machine or on the switchboard? Why can't clerical workers spend time learning more about their department, or trying out other jobs? Because American corporations, and the nonprofit organizations that imitate corporations, insist on rigid hierarchies, keeping the top people always on top.

In fact, companies spend a lot of money and effort just to preserve this hierarchy. They invest thousands of dollars in office decor that emphasizes the importance of some people and the unimportance of others. One insurance worker described her office as "very class-structured. The very biggest honchos, like the president and vice president, work in a section called mahogany row because they put all this mahogany paneling and this orange grass paper up on the walls, and they have central air conditioning in there, and doors on their offices, and differently colored chairs and sofas, and even their secretaries have nicer desks than everybody else's secretaries. You can walk in and look at someone's chair and know what their position is."

This is not a company whim. Giving people the appropriate symbols of importance is a serious part of office management. One textbook even suggests desktop dimensions for people at each level, from "top executive" (76 x 36) to "junior clerical" (42 x 30).[52] Titles, attitudes, assumptions about people — all go along with the differences in desk dimensions. Personal secretaries are trained in status rituals. A specific telephone procedure is used to call a person who is above your boss in the hierarchy. These things are serious parts of office life because they help maintain the psychology of control from the top.

Management claims that the division of jobs in the office has to be this way for efficiency. It may be more efficient for management's goals to have most people doing boring, dead-end jobs. Does that mean it should happen?

Most Americans have been taught not to expect their jobs to be anything more than a means to a paycheck. But many people today are questioning this assumption, and insisting that the quality of their experience on the job *should* be taken into consideration. Work *could* be reorganized to be interesting and varied, and to promote the personal growth of the employees through learning more and having more say in what they are doing. Most people would probably feel that's more important than the ability of the company to make as large a profit as possible.

---

14. WE'RE LIKE ONE BIG HAPPY FAMILY HERE

Management would like office workers to feel that everybody's in this together — that what's good for the company is good for you. But the fact is that everybody's in it on very different terms. The president of the Boston office of one major insurance company made $217,692 in 1972. That year the average salary for a class-C file clerk was $88.50 a week in the Boston insurance industry.[53] Of course, the difference is not just money. It's partly prestige. But most of all, it's power. A small group, usually white and male, makes all the decisions from the top — decisions that shape the working lives of employees.

In a real family, some people have more power than others too. But supposedly parents love their children, and exercise power to benefit them. Corporations are different; first, because the employees are adults and should not be treated like children, and second, because employees are not loved ones, but, in the eyes of most employers, "labor costs."

Every personnel policy in the office, from coffee breaks to salaries to job descriptions, is decided by management with this in mind. This is why companies won't allow real "democracy" on the job. As one economist explained, "By its nature the corporation is not primarily concerned with workers' lives . . . Rhetoric about a community of interest cannot obliterate elemental conflicts between employers and employees.[54]

In a profit-making company, management must try to make as much profit as posible in order to compete with other firms. They have to try to spend as little as possible for employees and get as much as possible out of them, just as they would with any other business expense, like equipment or building space. Nonprofit companies have a different set of pressures, but they result in the same way of thinking about employees. Because our whole economy is based on profit-making, nonprofit organizations, like colleges and social services, have a hard time getting money. People who run these organizations always face big demands for services with inadequate funds. To deal with these pressures, the easiest thing to do is copy the profit-making companies — squeeze as much as they can out of employees for as little money as possible. These decisions are not made because management is made up of malicious people. The pressures are built into the structure of a capitalist (profit-based) economy.

This *doesn't* mean the situation is hopeless. Employees can win real changes in their work lives and salaries. It *does* mean, however, that the way our economy is presently set up forces employees to fight for what they need and want. Otherwise they will be passed over. Traditionally, people who work in offices have been reluctant to organize or protest. But now office workers are beginning to stand up for themselves on the job, finding new rewards, and new dignity.

3

Origins of the
Current Movement

One day in 1965, seventy-five women clerical workers descended on the State Personnel Board in Sacramento, California. They did not look like typical 1960's protesters. All were state employees, many middle-aged. But they had just heard the state's decision on their annual pay raise — two percent — and they were angry.

In 1970 a group of three hundred clerical workers stuck out a six-month strike against the Fruehauf Trailer Company in Detroit. They were demanding a union contract, a pay raise, and an end to sex discrimination.

That same year, in Boston, secretaries working for a downtown accounting firm met and decided to divide up their work in a way *they* thought was fair. They wrote a statement to their male bosses, explaining what they felt was wrong with the traditional secretary's "servant" role, and circulated a memo changing office procedures. It outlined what they would do and what they refused to do. After a campaign of individual talks to pressure the women, the bosses finally fired one of them. But several years later she became one of the founding members of "9 to 5," a city-wide women office workers' organization.

In the August, 1972, issue of *Ms.* magazine, Susan Davis wrote: "Women's caucuses are known to exist in over 100 companies, including Polaroid, Blue Cross, Atlantic Richfield, General Electric, Scott Foresman, Readers' Digest, Celanese and AT&T." Her article also mentioned women employee groups at CARE, the American Civil Liberties Union, Newsweek, Time, and the Ford Foundation.

One day in 1973, five clerical workers in an insurance office in Hartford decided they'd had enough. Supervisors from another part of their department had been harassing them and constantly checking on their work. The men had been particularly hard on the only black member of the group. Nervous but determined, the five clerical workers marched into personnel and demanded that the harassment and racism stop. Their protest was successful. The supervisors were told to leave the women alone, and they were not punished for protesting. "We knew they couldn't afford to fire five people," said one member of the group.

In 1974, in a Boston investment counseling firm, a group of secretaries successfully pressured their employers into creating a maternity-leave policy. One of them was pregnant, and had been offered a maternity leave with many restrictions. The group contacted anti-discrimination organizations, did research on laws and other firms' policies, and wrote up a proposal that maternity leave be treated like leave for any other temporary disability, with full benefits. To their surprise, their employers accepted the proposal.

In 1975, secretaries in a Chicago law office forced the attorneys to listen to *their* ideas when planning a new office. The firm had ordered new desks which would have had secretaries sitting two together within a small area, enclosed by partitions on three sides. When most of the secretaries signed a petition protesting the new desks, the attorneys ordered the desks redesigned to give the secretaries more room. One of the women pointed out that this action involved something more important than desks: "I really believe this is the first time the Administrative Committee actually sat down and discussed secretaries as people. And the fact that they actually called the architects and told them to go back to the drawing boards is a very important thing."

These incidents don't seem very important in themselves. Hundreds of small protests like this happen every year in offices throughout the country. But, added together, they *are* very important, for they signify a growing trend in America — the beginnings of a movement of office workers. These protests are signs of a new spirit: a refusal to submit quietly to whatever the boss decides, a growing determination to stand up for themselves.

Starting slowly in the late sixties, office rebellions have become more and more frequent. Somebody decides she's had enough. A man is *again* promoted over the heads of more qualified women. The company comes out with *another* arbitrary change in the rules. Or the long frustrations of low pay and lack of respect just boil over.

Businessmen's publications have started to warn employers of "increasing restiveness" among white-collar workers.[1] An opinion poll described in the *Harvard Business Review* showed that the office workers surveyed no longer bought the myth that management would take good care of them and that these workers had a much more negative impression of their employers than office workers surveyed in the past. They were dissatisfied with their salaries and no longer believed that their employers were fair or responsive to employee opinion.[2]

Magazines for secretaries themselves reflect a new range

of concerns. The October, 1974, issue of *Today's Secretary* includes a report on office-worker protest groups, complete with color photos, as well as articles on sex discrimination and non-sexist language.

In response to growing office activism, some unions are beginning to show more interest in organizing office workers. A few have held special conferences on white-collar organizing. Some have hired former clerical workers as organizers, to bring new office groups into the unions.

Historically, clerical employees have been slow to protest or organize. Clerical work was considered, for many years, a good job — for a woman. The pay was all right — for a woman. As long as women accepted the division of work into men's and women's jobs — as long as they *expected* to earn less because women *deserved* less — the employers of clerical workers had it easy. Their employees were told to be grateful for what they had and not to complain. That was just the way things were.

Little girls were also brought up to be "good" — to obey the authority of parents, teachers, and eventually husbands. By the time they got to the office, obeying and trying to please authority was already a habit. It wasn't feminine to complain or rebel.

Besides, a woman's "real" life wasn't at the office at all. It was at home, with her children and husband — or it was trying to get a husband. Women felt this way partly because of conditioning and partly because the alternatives of the office or factory weren't very attractive. When work was over, a woman wanted to go home. Besides, she usually *had* to go home, to her second job, of housewife. The home, men, and children kept pulling women away from jobs. The typical pattern was to work a few years at a time, interrupted by duties as housewife and mother. Many women didn't want to get involved in trying to change their jobs because they expected to leave them soon. And anyway, it didn't seem quite right to go out alone at night to a meeting and leave your husband with the kids.

In fact, there have always been many women who worked all their lives. Today more women work more years, and, as we have seen, the patterns of their lives are changing. And the growth of a women's movement has led office workers, like women everywhere, to take another look at their lives. That often means accepting the fact that this office is where they are — at least for now — and that if they want to improve it, they'd better do something.

In the past, many office workers were reluctant to rock the boat because they felt that no matter how bad the office was, they were lucky to be there at all. Over the years the "privileges" of office workers have slipped away. And with them is going the idea that office workers are somehow "better" — higher in status than blue-collar workers — and "above" organizing or protest. The traditional office worker hoped for raises and promotions from the boss's recognition of "individual merit." As offices grow larger and more impersonal, this chance seems less promising than the gains to be won by the strength of a group.

Another big obstacle to group action is fear. One union organizer reports that he gets calls every day from insurance company employees about unions. But the callers are afraid to leave their names. The fear of being hassled or fired — or even of disrupting relationships with people you have to work with all day — often keeps people from protesting on the job. Of course, these fears sometimes are warranted. One of the main reasons office workers haven't organized more is that their employers try so hard to stop them. But as people start to question old assumptions, their anger grows. And as they see other people questioning, they begin to see a hope for change.

One university secretary thought that much of the growing activism had to do with the women's movement, "in the sense that it made women aware that they were people doing important jobs. And the whole trend now towards careers, and the fact that women will be working for a long period of time has something to do with it. Women, I think, in the last couple of years, irrespective of how long they plan on working, are just really starting to pay attention to their health plans and pension plans. Five years ago, if a woman had a pension or a health insurance policy, she'd take it home and give it to her husband and never even look at it. But *now* they're starting to look and say, 'Hey, I don't like this,' or 'This is good.' "

Another university secretary said simply, "I'm a product

of the sixties — fighting for independence and knowing it's a battle all the way. I know that those who have power are not going to give it up willingly."

Margie Albert, a former secretary who is now a union organizer, wrote, "The Women's Liberation Movement appears to be on the threshold of a second phase — when feminist consciousness reaches beyond white, middle class women . . . A clear sign of the new awareness felt by the so-called typical woman is the way office workers are asserting themselves. For there's nothing quite so typical as a woman who is a secretary, typist, clerk, or keypunch operator . . .

"Now . . . we see the beginning of a potentially powerful alliance between the labor movement and the women's movement.

"Employers who thought their 'girls' were immune to the subversive ideas of 'feminism' find those women suddenly making demands — to be treated with respect, to earn more money, to define their duties, to advance, and to get fringe benefits that other workers enjoy." [3]

As this awareness and assertiveness have grown, office workers in many companies, universities, and government agencies have gone beyond one-shot protests to form more permanent organizations. Some stay small, focusing on discussion and "consciousness-raising," like the six-member Clerical Support Group at the University of Minnesota. Some grow into large, permanent organizations, like the AT&T Alliance for Women in New York, or Federally Employed Women, which is now a national organization. Others look toward unionizing as a way to gain more strength. The groups put out literature, hold classes and conferences, and use public pressure, demonstrations, legal action, and even lobbying to promote the interests of women in their workplace.

Women who work for an Eastern university, Polaroid, the City of Boston, and a major New York publishing house have all formed women's groups in the past few years. These four particular groups and the reactions they have encountered are all very different. Together they give an idea of the possibilities, problems, and personal feelings involved in forming groups of women employees.

AN EASTERN UNIVERSITY

In the fall of 1973, a clerical group called WOW (Women Office Workers) held a conference in New York City. Several university secretaries saw a notice of the conference in Ms., and went down to see what it was all about. One of them said later, "I can never forget what Margie Albert was talking about at that conference. She was saying there are millions of office workers in the United States, and virtually none of them are organized. How strong we are in terms of numbers. And how stupid we've been because we haven't organized."

When they returned to the university they continued meeting and eventually formed a committee to protect the rights of office workers. The group is typical of many springing up on campuses across the country.

Lucille: I worked in the elementary education department, and there were several of us who used to talk about our work. We didn't really know if we wanted to go union or what, but we knew that we wanted to somehow get the secretaries organized into a group to effect changes. So we finally got together with two other people in the Ed. School and started meeting.

Stephanie: I think the reason I got involved is because I realized, after working in offices for *years,* that they couldn't care less if I walked out of this office tomorrow. Suddenly you think, "Why should I be treated this way?" You're proud of your work and yet you realize nobody else thinks it's important. After feeling hurt, I began to get involved with raising my consciousness and raising other people's consciousness — saying, "Hey! I'm important!" That's the main reason I got involved. Plus I thought the pay was lousy!

Lucille: First we just sat around and complained. Then we formulated a questionnaire — this was all very underground — and sent it out to what we thought were most of the staff, because we don't have a mailing list. And then we announced that we would have a big meeting in the chapel. There were about two hundred people there. After that we started small weekly meetings, and we've had a series of administrative people come and talk to the group.

A lot of people thought that we couldn't evolve any changes. But we've been around for about a year and half now, and we *have* effected changes. For instance, they were going to have child care just for graduate students. They had an open hearing, and we really feel that if we hadn't spoken up and said, "Hey, we want some child care," they would have had it for the graduate students and faculty only.

And we had the insurance guy come and talk. The maternity plan was really outrageous. The only way you could be covered for maternity was to have your husband on your policy. And single women — of course not! We were really giving it to him left and right, and the company said, "no, blah, blah, blah, no!" And then, funny thing, in the middle of August, they changed their policy. Single women now *can* get on the policy. Married women do not have to have their husbands on it.

Now we want to approach the faculty budget committee, which decides who gets what money for raises. We think that not only secretaries, but physical-plant workers, housekeepers, all these people should have representation on these boards, instead of just the elitist faculty members. The faculty have already requested a fourteen percent raise, so we figured, *we* will ask for a fourteen percent raise! And we're just going to go at it — the fact that we have a lousy pension plan, the fact that we have an inadequate health plan, and the fact that we're just getting ripped off!

The university doesn't like any news going out against them. They don't want the people that leave all their millions to them to find out about things that ruin their image. And we're at the point now where the people in Personnel are very much aware that we exist, and they are somewhat afraid of us, in the sense that they know the potential power we wield. I mean, if nine hundred office workers went on strike one day, the place would fold.

At this point we're not yet ready to decide whether we want a union or not.

Helen: We had this guy from one local come to speak to us, and I really think this turned me off a lot. He wanted us to go out and get people to sign union cards. At that point we were very new. I can't see myself going up to someone I don't even know and saying, "Hey, why don't you sign this card?" in so many words. It's hard enough to convince people that there are inequities.

Lucille: I think the thing that turned us off was the fact that we felt we could get some hints on organizing from this person, but his whole concern was making the buck and bringing us into the union. But then we did approach an organizer for the Distributive Workers of America, and she didn't have that approach at all. She really was concerned about our organization.

CITY WOMEN FOR ACTION

Julie is a former employee of Boston City Hospital. She is now on the staff of City Women for Action, an organization of women who work for the City of Boston. She became active after a personal experience with sex discrimination — applying for a management job for which she felt qualified, and seeing the job given to a man. As a result, she filed a sex discrimination complaint.

I had helped set up the office with the guy who left, so I knew I could do the job. Two months before posting the job opening, they started interviewing people on the sly — all men. I got four other women, besides myself, to apply for the job, and this one guy they had been interviewing all along got the job. He had connections.

But how can there be sex discrimination if everything is regulated by civil service?

In different ways. First of all, men and women tend to start out in different kinds of jobs. A lot of women go into clerical work. If they come in at entry level they have to type fifty words per minute and might have to take shorthand. Entry-level requirements for the jobs most men take don't have such high requirements. And the woman can't have any kids. They don't come right out and say that they're not going to hire you because you have kids, but they don't hire you. Then, the men, even though they're in the same pay grades, move up faster. Women are classified as clerical. An administrative secretary is actually doing management duties, but when she applies for any management job, they say, "You're clerical, so you're not qualified to take that job."

What action has your group taken?

Well, the hospital women, the library, and the Boston Redevelopment Authority women filed sex discrimination suits [in August, 1974]. Then we had a lunchtime rally to announce the complaints and two hundred people were there. No sooner had I got back to my desk from speaking at the rally than [a top administrator] was on the phone to me, using my first name, saying, "What's going on, why didn't you come to me and tell me about this?" Well, we *tried* to go through him and he didn't do anything about it!

The hospital's affirmative action plan was bullshit. They were able to balance the statistics in such a way that it looked like they were really complying. I was one of the people who worked on it! The decision was made to make the figures look good: they put different job classes in different categories. It was amazing the way they did it.

Now there's a City Women for Action group at Boston City Hospital. A lot of people come to meetings with problems that have to be resolved right then. One woman starts talking and somebody else says, "That happened to me, even worse." You get a lot of help from other women who have been in that same situation. Then, if they like, we will go into the workplace with them. Or if they want to file a complaint, we will give them the entire background, how long it takes and everything, and we will stand by them. We will go down to one of the anti-discrimination agencies with them. The agencies try to get both parties together and straighten things out. If they have to go to court, it takes forever. The first BRA

[Boston Redevelopment Authority] suit took four years.

It's funny when you think of the busing situation that's going on here now, and then you go to the meetings we have at the hospital. There are women from all age levels and color. They just sit around and talk to each other and say basically the same things. There's no "You're black and I won't sit next to you," there's nothing like that. They really respect and treat each other very nicely. Once they've joined a group and they've started talking about their problems, they see that they all have these problems. It used to be "Oh, they are getting all blacks in here, the blacks are getting all the jobs." But once they've sat together and talked together they realize that blacks aren't getting *all* the jobs — they're getting all the *lousy* jobs.

POLAROID WOMEN'S GROUP

One of the main legal tools for women on the job is af-firmative action. The federal government requires any company with federal contracts to file an affirmative action plan about its personnel policies toward women and minorities. The company has to promise more than just equal treatment in the future. It has to show plans for overcoming the effects of past discrimination, with programs like job posting and training classes. The company is also supposed to set goals and timetables stating how many women and minorities it will have in each type of job (goals) by a certain date (timetables). For instance, in a recent affirmative action settlement, the Bank of America had to promise that forty percent of its officers would be female by 1979.

The Polaroid group was similar to women's groups or caucuses in many companies. These groups started because employees felt that companies wouldn't enforce these affirmative action plans unless they were actively pressured to do so. Susan Ells describes how the Polaroid group won its demands.

The Polaroid Women's Group really is dead now, but the things it stood for are being implemented — like goals and timetables, and equal maternity benefits for single as well as married women. We got them to treat the temporary disability of childbearing the same as they treat a broken leg. And they put a Women's Coordinator in the Equal Opportunity Office. Those were the four main things the women's group was pushing for. It took us about a year.

Polaroid's whole idea was participatory management, for a couple of reasons. Number one, the company is not unionized — "and we like to keep it that way." So to keep unions out you must be super-good to your employees. You give them better than average salaries, better benefits. But you can only afford to do this if you are panicked about unions, which Polaroid seems to be, and also if you have a lot of money. I mean, look at Xerox, IBM, Polaroid — none of them have any unions. Besides, Polaroid is the creation of one man, Doctor Land, who is a very idealistic guy.

So how did Polaroid respond to the Women's Group?

Well, we started making these requests to the management committees. We were saying "You'd better change the wording on all the policies so that it is he/she," "You have to pay for the temporary disability of childbearing," and "Did you realize that the employment applications are going against the federal guidelines?" Then the manager of one of the other women, and my manager, said, "The two of you can spend x amount of time of your working day dealing with the whole women's issue."

Then one of the division managers proposed to us that we form task forces on the issues and do reports and present all the aspects of the problem to management. So that's when we got lots of women involved. We had a task force on the status of women. They allowed us to write a computer program, so when we got our data back, we had more information about the status of women than management ever knew about. We had stuff like the average pay of women, and the salary ranks, and the average number of women per position. It was magnificent.

We also had a policy task force to look at corporate policies. The third task force was "practices," which covered everything, like the fact that the company would hire women for certain jobs and men for certain jobs. You'd have clerical training programs and have only women in them, and mechanical training programs that had only men in them — so the training programs didn't really change sex discrimination, they just enhanced it. And then we had a task force on action education and we held management awareness sessions. And then one on compliance with the federal guidelines, which listed nineteen things the company should do. The first one was setting goals and timetables for women. That was all done and written out and presented to management.

Then they came up with a written statement that said our presentation was magnificent, and they were going to give single women the same benefits as married women, and pay for the temporary disability of childbearing, and open up the position of equal opportunity coordinator for women. *However*, in terms of goals and timetables, they did not think that was appropriate at this time.

Two months later Polaroid was investigated because one of the federal agencies was about to award Polaroid a two-million-dollar contract. I don't know what happened, but the company didn't seem to respond enthusiastically, and Washington sent a letter asking it to show cause in the next thirty days why it couldn't establish goals and timetables, or it would be taken to court.

I had just gotten the new job as Equal Opportunity Coordinator for women. And so, six months after being told that goals and timetables were inappropriate, I am sitting there with the corporate attorney and the head of Equal Opportunity, and we are writing like mad. We're describing the *model* affirmative action program, with goals and timetables, for women and blacks. And here is the same manager coming into the room saying, "Magnificent, magnificent!" That shows what the threat of bad publicity, the threat of losing a contract, can do to turn people's heads around!

A NEW YORK PUBLISHING COMPANY

The women's group at one major publishing house in New York cooperated with several state and federal agencies by providing evidence of sex discrimination at the firm. When they held their first public meeting in October, 1974, another employee group requested an election for a union. The following week, without notice, more than one hundred and fifty employees were laid off. The company claimed it was because of economic difficulties. The union and women's group activists feel that the layoffs were in retaliation for their organizing.

Liza had been working in publishing for many years, and was a department head and vice-president at the time of the firings. She was also a leader of the women's group.

We came to the conclusion that it was part of the personnel policy to keep employees uninformed as to what policy really is. Each supervisor or division could do pretty much whatever they felt like doing. One of the aims of the women's group was to force the corporation to make its policies clear to everyone. Once women from all different divisions began meeting, the company's inconsistencies began emerging in what seemed to us to be a pattern of discrimination against women.

Then around January of last year [1974], we began gathering complaints. We would have members write out their complaints and discuss them at the meeting. It was a terrific way of raising people's consciousness. A lot of people feel that they don't have any clear cut complaints until they start putting things down on paper. When they start hearing the nature of other people's complaints, their own start coming into focus. At the same time, we urged our members to reveal their salaries to the group. This was hard for a lot of our women, but it is a very important fact-finding and consciousness-raising step.

Many of the women in our group were terrified of losing their jobs. We felt we had to stay more or less undercover until we got legal protection. But our existence spread through the grapevine from floor to floor among women employees, and we knew that some male supervisors knew about us too. We were getting nearly one hundred women attending some of our meetings during Wednesday lunch hours. We didn't have a really big open public meeting until October ninth. Over two hundred women attended. That was five days before the firings. We'd been operating for almost a year.

No management today is going to fire someone and say that the reason she was fired was because she was a member of an activist women's group. But there is always a way they can fire you. I thought I was virtually un-fire-able. I'd been with [the company] for thirteen years, had been an assistant vice-president for the past five and a half years, and had just been promoted to a full vice-president. What they had to do to fire me is almost unbelievable, but they did it. They had to say there was no longer a need for my department and they had to wipe it out.

Most of the people they fired in October had low seniority, had not been with the company for more than a year or two. But when you looked at the people who had been with the company for more than two years, you found almost consistently that they were either union organizers or active in the women's group.

It was unfortunate that retaliation came right now when it's so bloody hard to get jobs, but oh, yeah, it was worth it for any number of reasons. Life is going to be much better for [the other] women, thanks to what the group started. The other thing is, I don't know how I could have lived with myself, having worked there all those years, if I hadn't been active in the group. The more groups of women who get together and do this, the faster we are going to see honest-to-God changes at all companies, not just publishing. And I think most of us who were really active in the group feel that it was a tremendously important experience.

Are there any clerical people who have been active in the women's group?

Not *leading* it, no. In fact, some women feel that the

group is too elitist, that there are more editors and professionals in it than clericals. And that's true. We didn't
actively solicit secretaries and clerks originally because
we felt they were too vulnerable. It's much easier for
management to fire them than professionals. We didn't
want to be responsible for women losing their jobs and
clericals were high-risk people. Along about April the
executive committee felt that we were strong enough to
start bringing in more clerical members, but I don't think
that part of it got moving fast enough. And then you get
into some interesting arguments with members who were
supervisors and felt that they were being discriminated
against by management, while other women in the group
who reported to these supervisors complained about
what poor supervisors these women were. We were trying
to develop a solidarity of all women at [the company] so
we would be able to cope with this kind of internal
problem, but it's bound to come up.

*What do you feel you learned from the women's group
experience?*

The only hope for women's groups anywhere is sticking
together and never considering your battle won. Never.
You really have to be a vigilante committee to ride the
company and make sure they really are complying with the
law and with whatever promises they give you. The only
way to do it is to really know what's going on within
your company — involve women from all departments
and all levels — pool your information and really ride the
company from all angles.

4

"We Have the Power of Women!"

After work on a June evening in 1973, representatives of management from twenty companies in Chicago sat and listened as three hundred angry women explained what it was like to work for them. The women quoted statistics that showed that women working in downtown Chicago made an average of $8000 a year less than men working beside them. They cited cases of women being paid less than men for the same work. They talked about the feeling of being trapped in dead-end jobs and treated with no respect. But the employers were seeing more than a protest of three hundred people. They were witnessing the beginnings of a new kind of activism by working women — the joining of employees from *many* companies into city-wide groups.

The women were organized by Women Employed, a group operating out of a small office in the downtown YWCA. The employers were members of the Chicago As-

sociation of Commerce and Industry, which had agreed to
this meeting after WE members had stormed indignantly
into their offices, armed with statistics that proved sex discrimination in Loop employment. To prepare for the meeting, WE had published its own statistical report.

Later that summer, as part of a campaign against a
"giant" in the food industry, Women Employed staged a
demonstration at a grocery store, demanding removal of
the company's products until it stopped discriminating
against women employees. In December, members crowded
into the offices of the State Street Council to protest sex
discrimination in downtown retail stores.

Through all of these early actions, Women Employed
was developing a style that combines direct action with
careful research and organizing. Since that year Women
Employed has grown into a substantial organization, in-
spiring the growth of similar groups elsewhere in the country: "9 to 5" in Boston, Women Organized for Employment (WOE) in San Francisco, Women Office Workers in
New York, Cleveland Women Working. These groups take
organization one step beyond single-employer "women's
caucuses," and organize working women on a city-wide
basis. While WE and WOE members include women in
lower-level professional and technical jobs, as well as clerical workers, and "9 to 5" is more strictly clerical, calling
itself the "Boston Organization for Women Office Workers," they all use pressure tactics to improve the treatment
of working women, and also help women organize within
their own workplaces.

Among their victories have been successful campaigns to
pressure employers into drawing up and implementing affirmative action plans. They have also pushed for stronger
enforcement of government anti-discrimination laws, and
have pressed for the enactment of new laws: to regulate
temporary employment agencies, to guarantee maternity
benefit rights to working women.

The groups have an impact beyond their numbers because they always seem to be in the news. At lunch-hour
confrontations with businessmen or government officials,
the press is always invited. Members appear on radio and
TV talk shows, and stand on downtown streetcorners,

handing out newsletters. One envious male official of a Boston union said, " '9 to 5' has the best publicity I've ever seen. It's incredible!"

On National Secretaries' Day in 1974, "9 to 5" and WE held lunch hour rallies that drew hundreds of women, with slogans like "Raises, not Roses!" and the announcement of a "Bill of Rights" for office workers. "What we're saying," a "9 to 5" rally speaker explained, "is that an office worker is not a personal servant, and she deserves to be treated with respect and to be compensated adequately for her work. And we *don't* mean a box of candy on National Secretaries' Day!" WE's first annual convention, said chairperson Darlene Stille, was "a show of force — that on a Sunday afternoon we could bring six hundred women downtown to the Conrad Hilton Hotel to affirm our commitment to winning our rights on the job. That's what it was. It was just fantastic!"

The women workers building these organizations come from many different jobs and industries, and bring a variety of backgrounds to the groups. Most have never been involved in anything like this before.

DARLENE STILLE

WE's chairperson, Darlene Stille, works for a publishing company. She says she used to go to women's liberation meetings, but got tired of just sitting around talking about problems. She refused to go to Women Employed meetings because she thought they would be more of the same. Then a friend got her to come along on an "action" (a confrontation with an employer) and Darlene became more interested. She started attending meetings, gradually getting more involved. The first big campaign she worked on was against a major food company.

Everyone was called a clerk. There were no job descriptions. And without specific descriptions, they thought they could get around the Fair Employment laws. You had women doing far more than a man and getting paid far

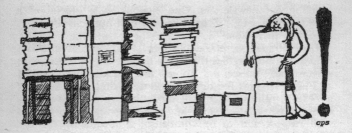

less, because of these broad, sweeping job categories. Secretaries were grossly underpaid.

One of our members was a secretary there. She had a master's degree in business administration and had come in looking for a management training program. They gave her this secretarial job and assured her that an opening would be available in six months in the training program. Six months came and went, and they said there wasn't anything. Meantime she found out that they'd hired five men and put them in — and she was still in the secretarial position.

I went to the Department of Agriculture and requested [the company's] affirmative action plans. They hadn't wanted to disclose them. The plan was two pages long and said they weren't planning on promoting or training any women for the upper-job categories of professionals or technicals or — God forbid — managerial employees. They said they couldn't possibly predict how many women would be hired or how many job openings they'd have — except in the clerical levels. They figured they were going to hire one hundred and eighty women for clerical jobs.

We finally pressured the federal government to send in a team of investigators from Washington. And they reviewed [the company's] affirmative action plan and found it wanting. And they issued something called a "show cause notice," which meant [the company] had to reply within thirty days at a hearing and show cause why it should not lose its federal contracts.

The government agencies are using working women's tax money. And it's not coming back to us in benefits unless we stand up and demand it. All the agencies which are responsible for overseeing these contracts should be doing their job and getting these companies to comply. We should not have to go to court when we're paying taxes to have these people do this sort of thing for us. That's their job.

Anyway, as a result of that investigation — which dragged on for nineteen months — all secretaries there were given across the board increases. Several women — I believe it was about twenty — were immediately promoted. Training programs were opened up to all the women there. And back pay was accorded to some women — in one case, two thousand dollars. The government said, "Unless you do this you are going to lose your federal contracts." And that's why affirmative action is one of the most important tools that working women have. I suppose the ideal thing to have in a company would be to unionize so that all the workers' rights were protected, and to have good, working affirmative action programs so that all the workers regardless of sex or race could be able to advance.

Why did you personally get involved in the campaign when you didn't work for the company?

I think it was the excitement of being able to do something instead of feeling so powerless. It was almost symbolic, at first. However, the organization now has expanded to where there are committees of banking women, insurance women, and secretaries, and committees for various companies and projects. And the feeling that now pervades the organization is that when women are in trouble over at a bank, the insurance women are going to come to help them, the secretaries are going to come to help them. Because we all know that the women in the banks are going to do the same thing for the rest of us when we're in trouble. So now we have a feeling of cohesiveness and unity in our common problems, whatever company we work in. I think the most significant thing we have done in the last two years is to show women that we are not alone in facing the situation — that now there are many of us and we're beginning to organize.

And the women in the Loop are beginning to understand
this principle: that the only way we are going to sig-
nificantly improve our working lives is by organizing
and by many, many women getting together. Large
numbers. All of the Loop, I hope, someday.

It's a very very brave thing that women are doing in
organizing around the job situation. We don't work for pin
money. It's our livelihood.

Has affirmative action been your main activity?

No. Secretaries in Women Employed have a very
strong committee that they've organized. Their first step
was to introduce, on National Secretaries' Day of 1974,
the Women Employed Secretaries' Bill of Rights. Secretaries want to be recognized for having the great skills that
they have. As one secretary said, "All the bosses in
the Loop could stay home for an entire week and no one
would even know it. Because it's the secretaries who
keep those offices running."

Over on LaSalle Street in Chicago there is a great
financial and legal district. Courthouses, big brokerage
firms, lawyers' offices. There are about five thousand legal
secretaries concentrated in that area alone. They all face
the problems of inadequate benefits and inadequate
pay. The Legal Secretaries Committee of Women Employed grew into a Legal Secretaries Council and is
beginning to organize secretaries company by company.

There are lots of companies in the Loop where we
have strong networks of women inside. In [an insurance
company,] for example, where the conditions were so
bad — click — a spark touched them off and all of a
sudden these women were coming together. The same
thing happened at one of the banks. A woman found out
she was not being paid the same as a man — click —
they started talking about it and all of a sudden the thing
mushroomed. Bingo — you've got a network of people
inside. Fortunately, Women Employed was on the outside
to relate to them and now we've got an even stronger
network inside. We're trying to build networks inside all
of the companies. We know that the only way permanent

changes are going to happen is if there's some sort of existing organization of employees within the company, whether it's a union or a less formal group to deal with specific problems.

I don't believe there was one of us in Women Employed who had ever made a speech or written a leaflet or engaged in any type of organizing before. We didn't know we could do it because we had never had a chance to do it. And it's one of the most pleasant surprises that a woman can have, to get up to do something new and find out that indeed she *can* do it! And we all give each other a great deal of support.

I was approached in June of 1973 and asked if I would like to gain experience chairing meetings. And I said, "No, I can't do that. I have never done anything like that before. There are lots of women more qualified than me, blah-blah-blah." I had absolutely no confidence because I had never done that before. So some women convinced me to try it out for a month. And here I am two years later.

It's given me a great deal more confidence in myself as a woman. I used to watch people on TV talk shows and wonder how they could ever be so articulate. How could people ever do that? But you realize there are certain things you want to talk about. And you research it and then all of a sudden — bingo — you're articulate. And it's been most exciting, watching this organization grow. And committees form. And new women come in. It's the most exciting thing I've ever done in my life.

Walk through the Loop here and you look up at the skyline and you see all these wealthy corporations that are so rich and powerful that it seems like you could never crack them. But when you look a little more closely, you say, "What are these buildings? What are they for? Who opens the mail? Who types their memos? Who keeps their computer systems running? The vast majority of people working in these companies are women. And without us, those companies wouldn't be running at all. So if *they* have the power of *money,* then *we* have the power of *women!*

THE WOMEN EMPLOYED BATTLE WITH
A CHICAGO INSURANCE COMPANY

Ellen, a clerical employee of a major insurance company in Chicago, started coming to WE Insurance Committee meetings when the group was pressing for an affirmative action plan at her company. Although enthusiastic about WE and their affirmative action victory, she and her fellow employees also experienced the limitations of pressure-group tactics and affirmative action strategy. Ellen explains how the company dealt with affirmative action, and how later developments pushed its employees toward the idea of forming their own union.

They brought the Social Security people in and they told them, "Hey, what's this? You're supposed to have an affirmative action plan! Get yourselves together!" So [the company] made one plan and the Social Security people turned it down because it was inadequate. They told them to make another one. OK. During this time some bosses were running around getting their secretaries to change the records, to falsify the records, really.

How did you find out about this?

Because there's this one girl, they told her, "We have to do a little something on the side, to whitewash things, to make them look all right." She refused to do it. She just told them that there were some things she would not do.

OK, so they made up affirmative plan number two. Social Security turned *that* down. When [the company] was supposedly on their *third* affirmative action plan, they sent around this memo saying that they had job posting, and they put the jobs on the board. But if you didn't have the same job grade as the job listed, you couldn't apply! And most women have low job grades. And OK, they post the jobs all right, but guess what they posted? Clerical jobs! Everything was typist, secretary, like that. None of the big jobs.

If a black woman quits, they're supposed to try to find a black woman from within the company to take that job within thirty days. OK. What they do is just procrastinate around, because if they haven't found anybody within thirty days, then they can pick the person they want.

So while we were running around trying to figure out what's going on with affirmative action [the company was sold]. And for economic reasons they decided to get rid of some of the people. They had lost quite a bit of money last year. OK, so they get rid of a few. But the *few* is growing!

They'll walk in and tell you, like at ten o'clock, "OK, you can get your stuff and go home." They don't give you notice. And whoever's the head of that department can get rid of whoever they want to. There's no policy whatsoever.

We figure the company's got a pretty good alibi — economics, you know. But we want some kind of policy that shows you *how* they're laying you off. We think that's only fair, but so far we've come to a dead end.

We were talking to a man from Social Security about three weeks ago. He said he would see if they could get them to draw up a plan about the layoffs. But there's one catch. What I seem to gather is that if the company comes up with a plan and the Social Security people accept it, they do not have to show it to the people that work for them!

Now we're going for a union. First we're going to pass out these cards and see how many responses we get, then we'll take it from there. We never pass things out in front of our own buildings! We always get other people from different companies to do it, and we go to their companies in return. If we get enough cards signed, that's when we really go into action. We cannot depend on the Social Security board. [The company] has gone for four years or more without an affirmative action plan. Why haven't their federal contracts been taken away from them?

Everybody seems to get the idea that Women Employed is a women's lib group. This is not women's liberation! It's for equal rights. If that's women's liberation, that's what we are. But we only want what's ours!

.   .   .   .   .   .

The strength of groups like Women Employed depends on organizing growing numbers of women workers. Their day-to-day work is mainly a slow process of involving, educating, and activating women. Phones in the small downtown offices are always ringing: "I saw your newsletter and I'm interested in joining," or "What can I do about the way women are treated in my company?" Staff people and older members spend many lunch hours meeting with individuals or small groups from different companies, answering their questions, making them feel welcome. New people are drawn in and involved — in "actions," in committee work, in learning and developing skills.

The groups' origins vary. WE was formed when Day Creamer, a YWCA staff member, saw so many working women coming in with employment problems that she began to feel they needed an organization. In the Boston area, a group of secretaries who had participated in the women's movement started meeting to discuss their personal problems on the job. After months of discussion they decided to form the activist organization that became "9 to 5." In San Francisco, a former union staff member pulled together a coalition of women's groups concerned with employment problems and moved from there to organizing unorganized women workers in WOE.

Today all operate with a handful of paid staff people and a large force of active members who devote many hours a week. Money, of course, is always a problem — for the staff's low salaries, for rent, for printing. Funds are scraped together from foundation grants, fund-raising gimmicks and, increasingly, from members' dues.

KAREN NUSSBAUM

Karen Nussbaum, a founding member and staff person for "9 to 5," describes some of the groups' activities during its first two years, and how participation has changed the women involved. She starts by describing what people learn from confrontations with employers.

People in Nine to Five understand now how an older man sitting behind a huge oak desk in a large room, with pictures on the wall of him shaking hands with President Nixon or John F. Kennedy and a secretary at his side, *uses* all of that to intimidate them. One of these guys *starts off* a meeting interrupting you, *starts off* by referring to you as girls, by intentionally forgetting your name, and making sure that you know his. People now understand these things as *tactics* and they're willing to develop their own tactics to counterbalance his. There are questions of real power and then there are questions of phony authority. You have to break through the phony authority to begin to fight the real questions of power.

One university group, after *eight months* of trying, finally arranged to have a meeting with the vice-president in charge of personnel. They arrived before he did. They had been to Nine to Five meetings and they were aware of these phony kinds of authority. The room was set up so that there was a huge desk in front of large windows, through which the sun was shining. So the leader of the group said, "I don't like to have the sun shining in my eyes, do you?" and everybody else said, "No, we don't." They all lined up *behind* the desk, so when the guy walked in, he was completely unnerved. They explained that it was because they didn't like the sun in their eyes. He had to sit in a regular chair; he didn't have the desk to protect him. And they started off the meeting with a psychological advantage.

How do people change personally from getting involved in Nine to Five?

Traudi says that she used to cry at her desk when her

boss would yell at her. Now she is a leader of her union group, and when her boss tried to harass her out of her job, she said, "No!" Her boss brought her in to have a personal meeting in which he intended to get rid of her, and she said, "I insist on having a witness." She did not lose her job; she got promoted. Judy McCullough says that she was known as "the quiet one" on her floor. She is now a staff person for Nine to Five and has become one of the key spokespeople.

It's partly a question of skills. Nobody ever taught us how to hold a meeting or to plan a series of actions that would win your demands from your boss. And then, through being in a group you can see things happen around you. You can see yourself be part of an organization that has an impact — that can eventually make big changes for working women. It's really seeing yourself as part of history.

The employees on campuses have been more active than any other industry. For instance, a group of clerical workers at Suffolk University had a couple of issues that they'd been worrying about for some time, but they were convinced that nobody else at work was interested. They went to a meeting of the Nine to Five Colleges Committee — twenty-five employees from twelve different campuses, who had come to talk about their common problems and explore solutions.

The next day the people from Suffolk went back to work and asked permission to address the committee that was making decisions about their salaries. Well, the answer was No. That afternoon they sent out a memo to everybody saying, "A meeting is going to take place where the decisions about *our* salaries are going to be made. We've been denied the opportunity to address that meeting. We urge every one of you to write letters to the board of trustees that will be making that decision." Within an *hour*, half a dozen people called them up to say, "Isn't this exciting? What can we do? Who should I write to?" They were galvanized. And this is because they understood that there are steps you can take, and saw that there were other people taking those steps.

We decided to focus on insurance because that's the

heart of the clerical workforce. Insurance and banking together employ nearly thirty percent of the clerical workers. And the majority of the women working in insurance are the women from the working-class neighborhoods. It's not like universities or publishing, which have large groups of out-of-state ex-college students.

When Nine to Five was in its early stages there were only about four people in the whole insurance industry who were involved with the group. I think that has to do with the fact that going to meeting after meeting to discuss problems is not something that working-class women do as readily as middle-class women. The women who work in insurance are more interested in *results* than in discussion. Also, the big insurance companies are very regimented. The repressive conditions keep people from going to meetings — management *tells* them not to go to meetings.

We developed a campaign, first of all, by doing research that proved the discriminatory working conditions for women in insurance. Then we demanded that the state Insurance Commissioner revoke the licenses of companies that discriminate against women. By taking complaints to the government, insurance employees weren't risking their jobs, as they might have been if they complained to their employers.

We were also working to get the women themselves involved, because the issue really is people taking control over their own lives — taking control over the working conditions that you face, and understanding that you have to fight to win something. Victories from the past that were won at great costs to large numbers of people, like minimum wage, child labor laws, overtime, social security, civil rights — all were won as a result of long, hard fights. But now they're just seen as "laws." They're "givens," to most people.

We started off by polling the clericals in the insurance companies. We stood in front of the companies in the morning, stopped people going to work, and said, "Do you think any one of the four following problems is an issue in your company?"

Well, we got a tremendous response. We took comments

written on the polls, wrote them up for each company, and handed them out again. People would get the leaflet and they would recognize themselves. They would say, "This is my company you're talking about — it says Liberty Mutual right on the top of this leaflet! Liberty Mutual is so important and the problems of the clerical workers are so important that you wrote a special leaflet for us." And they got friendlier and friendlier. They were seeing that their comments were being *used*. There was a *result*. And a real identification with a growing struggle developed among the women in the companies. Slowly we picked up more and more contacts. People would call us on the phone and start coming by the office. It's been a slow and steady and *successful* development.

We would like to see the Insurance Commissioner adopt the proposed regulations we have drawn up. But the power of the Insurance Commissioner is limited. He can threaten to suspend or revoke licenses, but he's going to have a hard time doing that because of the power of the insurance companies. Also the issues that he can address are limited to those that are covered by the law. There's no law against low pay. It's the prerogative of your boss to pay whatever he wants. So in order to begin to address those very fundamental problems of pay, of distribution of work, of decisions about the way your own department is run, people are going to have to form stronger, more permanent groups within the companies. For some that may mean union organizing.

Why didn't you organize a union instead of Nine to Five?

Well, at first we thought unions were bad. We thought they were corrupt, just out to get money for their officials. We thought they regimented the working conditions. We thought they weren't democratic.

When we started, the options we had weren't good. The union people scorned women. They didn't care to take the time with us women, who didn't know *anything* about unions. I mean, "union," "collective bargaining," "contract negotiations" — these words didn't mean anything to us. It wasn't like "refrigerator" or "electric light" — things that we had grown up with that were very familiar concepts. These were completely alien.

But Nine to Five did begin to feel that unions were necessary to do the best job for people at a particular workplace. People need to have an organization that negotiates about conditions of work, and the only organizations with the power to do that are unions. And, at the same time, we began to sense that we had the ability to create an alternative, a different kind of unionism. That there was a movement of women office workers — just beginning — but a real movement. We could see that people who came to Nine to Five started off quiet, but then became vocal and confident. These people are not going to become quiet again. If they join unions, they're going to be vocal in their unions. And if this is a movement of the substance and power and impact that it seems like it might be, well, then it could transform the unions!

5

The Next Step:

A Union?

As office workers organize, many move toward the idea of unionizing. One woman changed her mind about unions while working as a secretary in a New York law office: "Most of us started out with a sort of anti-union attitude because we felt that a union shop where everybody *had* to join would deny your right of free choice. But we tried all the other means — petitions, meetings, pressuring management to make certain changes. We saw that if we didn't have any clout, we didn't get respect from the employer."

A group of office workers at a university in central Massachusetts came to the same conclusion. "People have had bad experiences with unions," a group member said, "but there's no way around it. You can't get money without irritating the university. You have to make a very clear break — you have to stand up and say, 'I am dissatisfied.' You have to see yourself as a worker and stop defining yourself in terms of the man you work for."

Maureen, a clerical worker at a large New York publishing house, talks about unions from a more personal point of view: "At one firm where I worked there was a woman who was sixty-three, I think. They were computerizing and they just wanted her out. They had somehow forced a lot of other people out, but she just wasn't about to retire. They forced so many other jobs on her that she would sometimes sit there and cry. They finally forced her to retire early. Oh, it was just shocking! Just shocking.

"How can we allow a dictator on any level of our lives? And that's how most of the people in offices work. When does the profit stop? When do we become more important than a profit? We should always be — *always* — more important than the profit, *I* think. Why did they ever stop sweatshops then? I mean, why just go from one degree to a lesser degree? It's just got to be! We *must* organize!"

These women are part of a growing movement toward clerical unionization. Unions report an increase in the number of inquiries they get from office workers. Statistics show a slow, steady rise in the percentage of white-collar workers in unions. In 1974 more new groups of white-collar workers voted in unions than in any other year since records were kept. The fastest growing unions are those with a high percentage of office workers — especially unions of public employees. And in all of the major "office industries," there are signs of increasing union activity.

On *university campuses,* so many groups of clerical workers are forming unions that organizers talk about it as a major trend. Inspired partly by the women's movement and partly by the unionization of faculty and blue-collar campus employees, the office workers have been forming their own grass-roots groups, which later usually affiliate with a national union — at Columbia, Harvard, Boston State, University of Michigan, Indiana University, University of Chicago, Berkeley, and UCLA, to name only a few.

Leslie Sullivan is a former lab technician at Harvard Medical School. She got together with other technical and clerical employees there and tried to get some kind of group going. The group eventually decided to join a union, and voted that Leslie be the staff person hired by the union as an organizer. During her campaign for the Distributive Workers of America at Harvard Medical School, she described why the group had decided to go union, and what it has meant for Harvard Medical School employees:

At Harvard, I think the initial thing that galls people most is the money. There's also a horrible dead-end *feeling* — this job is dead-end and everybody knows it. You're surrounded by going-places people, people that have succeeded or are succeeding. And yet I think it's very clear to employees that they are probably just as bright and just as sharp as the people who are around them. I think at Harvard there are a few exceptionally bright professors, but that on the whole they're not an exceptional group. Sometimes I don't know how they got where they are.

It seems like the employees do everything, and professors spend most of their time trying to get money from the government. All the real work in the labs and offices is done by the employees. And yet their work is never recognized as valuable. I think it could be different. If you make more money, people are going to view you with more respect. They should open up those jobs, create a ladder, so that people would know that within a certain amount of time their work will be reviewed and they can go on — or tell people what the exact qualifications are for higher-level jobs, so that they know if they take courses they will be promoted or will be recognized with more responsibility and more pay. Right now there's no review. And in many cases there's nowhere to be promoted to.

How did your group get started?

A group of women, mostly faculty, put up notices saying that women were meeting to discuss affirmative action. I went to the meeting. We decided that we would form the Medical Area Women's Group. The employees formed an active subdivision of that group and it just sort of grew from there.

We decided very early to drop affirmative action as a waste of time. The only people who are helped are, maybe, faculty because there are so many more men than women on the faculty. In our job categories, we're basically all women, and affirmative action doesn't have any provision for a situation where the *entire* class of women is being discriminated against.

One of the things we accomplished was getting a Committee on the Status of Women established and funded by Harvard. The thing that amazed me though was that employees seemed to have much more political ability than faculty and students. Students were disinterested, and faculty were the most naive group of women I've ever seen. They just didn't know how to get things done. They didn't even know how to relate to each other. They never really had common goals. I don't think they could ever separate it from their personal interests, whereas the employees always saw their interests as the same. There was no competition. We were a close-knit group.

Anyway, the original employees group died. Most people left, partly because it got to be summer, when interest always drops off. Also, we had no focus. We never mentioned unions. We thought people would be frightened by the word "union."

But the next year I met a secretary who was pretty interested in going ahead with a union. By this time I was getting pretty tired, but she was all enthusiasm. So we basically started this union with two people. We started writing a newsletter and called a meeting of the people from last year's mailing list. We got together a core group of about fifteen people and called ourselves the Harvard Medical Area Organizing Committee.

We did a lot of research on unions and eventually chose the Distributive Workers of America. We chose very carefully. We didn't want to be swallowed up. We talked to a lot of workers who were in that union in other places to find out how it actually was in practice. One of our strong points was that we were very well organized within our own group before we called in the union. We knew what we wanted and that made it much easier for us to deal with the union.

One of the things people say about the union is, "No matter what, it's been so nice to get to know other em-

ployees." At Harvard everyone is very isolated, and to
finally be together and do something together has been a
tremendously positive experience. And you get people
involved. It's been a tremendously broadening experience
for a lot of people. Some of the people who have become
involved in our committee have never done anything
similar to this before. All of a sudden some people realize
that they're very good at talking to people. People can
write who never realized they could write before. Some
people are blossoming in things they never had any idea
they were good in.

Also I think the drive has given employees a little more
confidence. For instance, one woman told me that she's
been having a problem with her boss for a long time. She
got along with him, but she wanted to be promoted and
he wasn't promoting her. Finally she went in and pushed
him, put it on the line, said she wanted what she wanted or
she was going to think about leaving. She told me she'd
gotten the confidence to do this, she'd been inspired to
do this, because of what the union was doing. It was
successful for her. She hadn't joined then, but about a
month or two later she joined the union.

·   ·   ·   ·   ·   ·   ·

During a successful organizing drive by the same union
at Barnard College, employees found that the experience
broke down some of the barriers between people. Mary
Wexford, who was a Barnard office worker during the
union drive, describes how this happened:

At Barnard there was a group of older women who had
been there for a long time. In the beginning, they had
the major complaints. They were the ones who were getting the lousiest pay. The younger people who were coming
in were getting higher pay, and that infuriated them. But
when you talked about a union, they got scared. They had
nice working relationships in their offices and they were
scared to death of losing their jobs, because they knew
at their age they weren't going to get another job very
easily. Later, as we got more and more involved in union-

izing, one of the issues we talked about was pensions, and they started to slowly filter back.

There was one older woman who was so quiet nobody even knew how she stood on the union. At the meeting when we took the strike vote, she got up and said, "Look. Not all of us need the money. But we have to think of the other people who work here who support themselves on what they make. And we also have to think about the pension that we could get, those of us who are about to retire. And we have to stick together. We can't refuse to fight for their issues, or they're not going to fight for our issues."

We were on strike in February, and it was bloody cold; we had blizzards every other day. Some of those older women with really serious health problems were out there on that picket line every damn day. A lot of it was due to this older woman's speech.

There's one woman who works in a one-person office. She has the bottom classification and doesn't belong there, but she never dreamed of fighting. She's been there eighteen years. This summer they waterproofed the walls of her office — it's in the basement — but they never finished the job. She was in there for weeks with plaster dust. She has asthma and she was going crazy. A light fell where she had been sitting three seconds before, and she thought, "What am I doing here? I've got a union. Let me go and fight this."

Now she goes to grievance meetings and tears people apart. She's great. She's sixty-three or sixty-four years old. She said to me, "You know, I stood outside in the freezing cold for eight days and I didn't even know why. Now I know what I stood out there for." Was that place painted fast! and cleaned up — and now they're going to hire a student to help her catch up on back work. They're going to have her job reclassified. It's beautiful to watch.

The *publishing* industry was shaken in the summer of 1974 by its first strike since the 1930's. New York employees of Harper and Row struck for seventeen days to demand a cost-of-living-increase agreement, re-evaluation of job descriptions, and improved health care plans. Harper and Row's independent Employees' Association was the only union in New York publishing at the time.

Shortly after the strike, the Harper and Row Employees' Association affiliated with the Distributive Workers' District 65, and became the core of an organizing drive that spread to Simon and Schuster and other New York publishing houses. Although most of the unionization in publishing is centered in New York, other publishing employees, such as the Bancroft-Whitney group in San Francisco, have also recently organized unions.

Peg is a Harper and Row editorial employee. She describes how the situation there built up to the strike:

Negotiations were going on and we passed the deadline. Management was using delay tactics, and their offers to us were quite insulting. The cost of living increases they offered amounted to 2.1 percent, which was ridiculous. They might as well not call it a cost-of-living increase. And in exchange for this they wanted us to give up profit-sharing, which we already had. This was their idea of negotiation! We offer you something terrible and in exchange you give up something. And it seemed that the attitude of management was very arrogant, very condescending, and it got people angry.

We did job actions. We wouldn't go back to work for the afternoon. It wasn't really striking. They docked our salary for that — two hours. And finally, nothing was happening, so we took a vote by secret ballot and it was overwhelming to go out on strike. After the vote it was like a sense of shock. Management still didn't seem to take things very seriously and they still refused to negotiate for about a week and a half. The state mediator contacted Harper and they finally said, "OK, we'll go into mediation."

What was it like being on strike?

It was very weird. First of all, you wake up in the morning and you don't have a job to go to, but you're not on vacation. You're just disorganized. I had made arrangements to get some freelance work to do. And I tried to set a pattern for myself. And then I was on a picket line three hours a day.

That was hard to do. I had just never walked on a line with a sign on me. I find it difficult to put myself on display like that. There you are in midtown Manhattan, which doesn't see too many picket lines, mostly women, and you get a lot of insulting reactions from people on the street. And then you see whether you can stop deliveries. It's tough to scream at a truck driver not to cross your picket line. But we did get pretty effective. There were some construction workers across the street and they weren't too happy with truck drivers that were crossing our line and they were yelling at them too.

We had no strike fund, but we raised enough so that people who were strapped could just come in and get money. All you had to do was come in and meet one person. She would not ask any questions; she would just give you the money, whatever you asked for. I had to ask for some money at the very end. I felt like, gee, there must be people who need it more, and the woman in charge of it said, "Don't be silly. It's money for everybody to take." So I did.

Do you think the experience of the strike changed you?

I was faced with the thought that I might get fired, that I might be out of work, that I had no money coming in. It was the first time in my life I had that.

But you also really got to know who you were working with, and you really felt a sense of solidarity. I hadn't known a lot of people, and I met them, enormous numbers of them, and got to know them.

Unions at most publishing companies go from the mail room clerk to the associate editor and sales people, which sometimes presents a problem, because people are different and what they want is different. But the power a union has is obviously the power of striking — that, they can hold over the head of a company. It was very humbling for me to realize that what really would cripple the company is the mail room walking out, and the building maintenance staff walking out, or the organized labor like the truckers not making deliveries because they were respecting the picket line. Secretaries walking out — that was crippling the company in the immediate. Now the fact that my work wasn't getting done was having a long-term effect. And it was embarrassing the company for people at my level to walk out — professional staff.

How did the industry-wide drive start?

On the picket line we had feminist solidarity days. We had publishing solidarity days, when everyone from the publishing companies came. And we had union solidarity days.

Then after the strike there were some people at Harper who had names of everybody from different publishing houses who walked the picket lines with us. Ever since the strike started there were industry-wide meetings going on. A number of unions started to talk with people from publishing houses.

The Harper group and the industry-wide group both set up committees to investigate union affiliation and we decided to go with 65 [District 65 of the Distributive Workers of America]. I thought they were really sincere about organizing, and they had a reputation for being good organizers. We had been the only union in publishing, and we felt that if we had an all-industry union, we would really gain strength. And I feel that, because I'm protected already, if I can do anything to help people who aren't protected, why not do it? And I think a lot of people at Harper felt that way. I just feel very strongly about people elsewhere organizing.

Public employees have been joining unions faster than any other group. The American Federation of State, County, and Municipal Workers (AFSCME), just one of the public-employee unions, is the fastest growing in the AFL-CIO, with about 1,000 new members a week. Its membership has tripled in the last ten years, in spite of the fact that the union rights of public employees are not protected by federal law, and are very restricted in most states.

In many places it's illegal for them to strike. "Without a legal guarantee of collective bargaining rights," one organizer explained, "you may never even get the chance to negotiate with your employer. In California, before the new collective bargaining law was passed, all you could do was make presentations to the State Personnel Board, who sat on a raised platform in a big auditorium. And you'd give a rational explanation of why you need more than a two percent raise, and then one of the board members would lean over and look down at you and say, 'For *clerical* work?' "

Now more and more public employees, many of them office workers, are organizing and pushing for bargaining rights. Traditionally, public employees have been organized in "associations." Kay Eisenhower, a clerical worker for Alameda County in California, explains that these associations "have a history of resisting unionism and of lobbying — trying to change through backdoor dealing and that kind of stuff rather than through organizing the membership to do anything. Definitely a conservative approach."

Recently, some of these associations have started to act more like unions, demanding collective bargaining and often affiliating with regular unions. Others find themselves voted out when a real union is voted in by the employees.

Faced with what they felt was a traditional inactive employees' association, Kay Eisenhower and a few friends decided to try to get a union to represent Alameda County clerical workers. They formed a group, published a newsletter, and contacted a local of the Service Employees International Union (SEIU) for help. After building up a big campaign to convince clerks to vote for the SEIU, the group heard that SEIU leaders had gone behind their backs and made an agreement with officials of the employee association. The association just suddenly became part of SEIU, with no employee election, keeping the same rules and officials. Even the women staff organizers assigned by the SEIU to work with the Alameda County group say they were not told of the deal beforehand.

One of these organizers said later, "They got sold out, but they didn't stay sold out." The organizing group, basing itself on their newsletter called *Clerk's County,* stayed together as a caucus within the union. Largely because of their efforts, the union is a real force in Alameda County offices. Kay describes how the idea of unions is spreading there:

One example I'm really fond of is a very pleasant woman in my office who is a very conservative person. She was on my list of "impossibles" for the union. But the day came when she got a bad evaluation for being slow. What had happened was that she worked in an office where they had the workload split up by alphabet. She had twice as many cases in her part of the alphabet as anybody else. She wasn't slow, she was overworked. She signed up with me that day and she's still in the union. We still disagree on a lot of issues, but she feels very strongly that people need union protection now, and she wishes her husband had it.

Various other people who I had also written off — and this really taught me a lot as to writing people off — came to me and signed up. They might have been conservative people, but every one of them at some point became the object of wrath of some management person. And they realized then that they needed help. I think that's why most people come to the union. The pity of it is that people don't come before. It's sort of like preventive medical care. If you nip it in the bud, you won't have the problem later on.

What are some of the main issues people are concerned about?

There's a lot that can be done just around the question of dignity on the job. Some of the specific ways of dealing with that are getting into the contract so many hours a week for stewards [employees who represent the union on the job] to work out grievances. Also, we're trying to get into the contract a procedure whereby grievances can be filed about supervisors' evaluations. And a union can publicize that they don't have to tolerate any kind of abuse based on sex, race, age, or whatever.

We're finding that there's a strong feeling among a lot of blacks, particularly in the hospitals, that they're denied equal treatment on sick leave for racial reasons. And women get asked questions in interviews that no one would ask a man, and that's illegal. A lot of women also feel that there's a strong problem with age discrimination.

When there's a real personality problem between a supervisor and an employee, as a steward, I will go to the boss and say, "I don't think this supervisor can give a fair evaluation of this employee because there's this personality problem." Several times I've gotten changes of supervisors based on that kind of intervention, although it's not clearly part of the contract. Some abuse is obviously based on racism and you can just threaten them with a suit.

We won a clause on maternity leave. It's not the best in the world, but people have job security, which is the most important maternity-leave demand. They are also allowed to use any accumulated sick leave or vacation time during the pregnancy-leave period. We're asking for fully paid maternity leave, and for paternity leave. There are also demands for more clerical input into reclassification.

I feel that clerks are now much more willing to fight for themselves than they ever have been before.

·   ·   ·   ·   ·   ·

Some black clerks in Alameda County have become active, not only in Clerks' County, but in a new black caucus among county employees. Black employees first started meeting together after one of them was allegedly attacked by a white member of the security force. They have since gone on to other issues, such as the county affirmative action plans.

The Black Caucus has met with administrators, reviewed the plans of each department, and pushed for more action against discrimination. "But, to me, the best thing that's happened," said one clerk, "is that there's never been any unity here before. I'd seen these people, but never sat down and talked with them about anything. Now we can appreciate each other better because we can understand each other's problems."

Across the Bay, clerical employees of the city of San Francisco began joining SEIU Local 400 in large numbers after that local hired two women, former clerical workers, as organizers. These two women helped city employees form their own "Clerks' Council" within the union. In the spring of 1974, strengthened by participating in the Clerks' Council, office workers took a leading role in a nine-day strike of San Francisco city employees. Maxine Jenkins and Louise Statzer, the two women organizers (who have since left Local 400), explained what happened during the strike and after:

Maxine: In 1974 the city Board of Supervisors offered the professional workers a 5 percent raise, some of them a 7.5 percent raise, and the clerical workers a zero-percent raise. Their rationale was that using the data from other public industries, the clerical workers of San Francisco were overpaid; they had a nice word for it, "over data." It didn't matter that the cost of living had gone up 14 percent. All that mattered was these papers that they shuffled around, these surveys.

We said, "We're not going to accept those surveys, because *all* clerical workers are underpaid, based on the fact that they are women. Throw those surveys in the waste can!" People were angry about it. So we hit the picket lines with furor and determination, and hung in there for nine days and nights. A lot of us laughed afterwards because, as many women of us as there were, we had lost more weight on those days and nights on the picket line than in all those diets that we had tried for years. It was like that — a women's strike.

We had also said we wanted money across the board, a dollar amount for everybody.

Louise: Five percent across the board, to somebody making $400 a month, is very little. But 5 percent to somebody making $2,500 a month is a heck of a lot more money.

Maxine: We didn't want a percentage raise so that higher-paid people got more. We wanted everybody to get the same raise.

Louise: We met with Civil Service, we met with the

Board of Supervisors, and they just absolutely refused to change their minds. So then the union took a strike vote and the membership ratified it.

It was a very high feeling that night. The room was just jam-packed. We had the ratification for the strike vote in this huge auditorium, and that, of course, was not enough, so we had to go to another auditorium. And *that* wasn't enough, so we had to go to another auditorium, and we had three floors of people there. Strikes aren't easy and people are apprehensive about losing their money, but I think people by and large realized that we had to really stick it out this time.

Maxine: All across the city, from sewage treatment plants to the Hall of Justice to a hundred different locations, the waterfront and everywhere, women were visible. It was quite apparent that women were the backbone of the strike.

Louise: The negotiating team, even though they would be hours and hours in negotiations, would come back to strike headquarters and then go out on the picket line. "We need somebody here, we need a picket over there," and they'd go out and picket, after being up half the night in negotiations. We put out strike-alert bulletins and had meetings in the strike headquarters. We also had a food wagon that went around with coffee and donuts to the people on the picket line — and hot chili! It was bad weather during the strike. It rained, it was cold, but everybody hung in there.

The clericals were in there doing a hell of a lot, because Maxine had been working with clericals all along, getting them organized. We have a Clerks' Council that we have organized within Local 400.

Maxine: We had decided to organize clerks into a sub-section within the local because women clerical workers weren't used to going out to union membership meetings. When you would go to a regular membership meeting of the local, most of the members were men. But when we held a special function for clerical workers, they would turn out — two hundred, three hundred — and the leaders of the union were absolutely bewildered by this. We saw that if we could get clerks together separately, then they could come into the big local from a position of power. So we formed a Clerks' Council, and it began to meet every month. We had a newsletter and all the articles were written by women clerical workers.

After the San Francisco city strike was over, the clerical workers had a new fight on their hands — to defeat "Proposition L." This was a referendum proposal to prohibit union bargaining for most low-paid categories of city workers, including clerical workers. Their wages were to be determined automatically by the wage surveys Maxine described. As she pointed out, this was really an attack on women, since clericals are low-paid largely because they are female. So, shortly after the strike, they mobilized to campaign against Proposition L — and won!

Maxine: It was during this time that we formalized our women's caucus. We met every other day. It was a life or death struggle for us. We published our message sort of like a letter to our sisters in private industry, and we leafletted in front of large banks and insurance companies before the election.

The women's movement was so beautiful. We called upon them for help, and they helped us leaflet. We formed panels and went and talked on radio shows, appeared on TV shows, wrote letters to newspapers, and had our own women's speakers bureau where we reached out to communiy groups throughout the city.

Each of us would encourage the others, because somebody would say, "I really can't speak in public. I'd be terrified." And then we'd say, "Come on, we'll have so and so who can speak in case anyone gets tongue-tied." By the end of the campaign we had polished public speakers among a whole range of women.

Telephone company clericals, the first office women to organize in private industry, have traditionally found themselves in "independent associations" which were in fact company-controlled. Now many phone company employee groups have left these associations to join one of the two major national unions organizing telephone workers — the Communications Workers of America, and the International Brotherhood [sic] of Electrical Workers.

Employees of New England Telephone and Telegraph voted to join the IBEW in 1971. In their first IBEW contract the top raise was $18.50 a week, in a company whose employees remembered typical raises of $2 or $3 a week. But money wasn't the only change. Pat Cote, a former phone company office employee and current union representative, describes some of the others:

Compare what we were working under, what the Federation [the independent association] called a contract, and what we were successful in negotiating in 1971, and it's like night and day. Pay, working conditions, job-bidding system, everything. Schedules, the whole bit. Even the way it's written. The Federation contract — you couldn't understand it. It was a real mess.

And they never went by the contract. No enforcement. The members were never given copies; only the Federation reps had them, and management. It was absolutely company-controlled. We never voted on a contract. I think the Federation reps were more obsessed with making an impression on management for themselves than putting their point across. I'm not saying they were all bad, but they seemed to have a little club going there.

.   .   .   .   .   .

Debbie, now an IBEW shop steward, explains how unionizing changed the atmosphere in the offices:

I think that people are feeling more equal. Management doesn't get away with favored treatment. And our promotions are by bidding, so it's really by seniority. Before, they would not post jobs, they would just tell the next person on the seniority list, "This is the job we have, do you want it?" If it was somebody that they didn't like, they could hold off the good job until that person got something else, and then fill the good job with the person they wanted. So they could manipulate it, even though it was supposed to be by seniority. Now they have to post the job on the board, and whoever wants it can bid.

.   .   .   .   .   .

New England Tel and Tel employees have also discovered, however, that just having a union does not solve all their problems. Ginny Cutting, a former telephone operator, now a union staff member, describes the problems that still remain:

Why did we get a better contract in 1971 than in 1974? The company needed us in '71 and they didn't need us in '74. Circumstances were different. Economic conditions.
We've got a contract. We can make sure that the company lives up to that contract, and if they don't, we can arbitrate. Unfortunately now it looks like the company has declared war on this union. It seems to me that they are doing everything they can possibly do, including breaking the contract, prostituting the grievance procedure, saying "no" to every single step, forcing us into arbitration, which takes three to six months if you're lucky. An arbitration case can cost the union a thousand dollars.
Unfortunately, a union's position is to react. The people look to the union as the be-all and the end-all, and it isn't. The union is only as strong as its people. And it's a

very, very bad time for people now. People say to me, "Stop them from laying me off," and I can't. The company has the right to lay these people off. The only thing that you can see to is that they do it according to the contract.

And there are problems that we can't get rid of — constant supervision, constant observation. They have the right to observation. They have the right to measure the work an employee does. We have the right to grieve it if we feel she's being treated unfairly.

I believe in unions. We're getting beaten now but I know that we can protect the people. I know deep down that they're better off than they were before.

Banking and insurance are the heart of clerical work. Between them these industries employ about one third of all clerical workers. They have been slower to organize, largely because of the repressive conditions in these giant white-collar factories. But office workers in these industries, as elsewhere, are beginning to move. When they are organized, they will contribute a great deal to the overall strength of clerical unionization. With a more powerful movement of organized office workers, some of the problems Ginny Cutting described may be easier to deal with.

In *insurance*, until recently, it was mostly the male agents who were organized, with the Insurance Workers International Union — a union that has traditionally ignored the mostly female clerical work force. Recently, however, the IWIU has organized a few groups of clerical workers, including those in three offices of Metropolitan Life, in California, Illinois, and Ohio.

Clerical workers in a few other insurance companies are represented by the Office and Professional Employees International Union (OPEIU) — from Northwestern Mutual Life Insurance in Milwaukee, to North Carolina Mutual Insurance Company in Durham, to American Income Life in Waco, Texas. Groups of Blue Cross and Blue Shield employees all over the country have made many attempts to unionize, mostly with the OPEIU — some successful, some not.

John, a clerical employee in a West Coast office of a major insurance company, tells how an active committee of employees successfully organized their workplace:

When you work at a place like this, it's really a sweatshop! I was a claims examiner and there were about 100 of us. Each of us had a minimum of five hundred claims a day. That's faster than one claim a minute. And you have to check the person's eligibility, the doctor's eligibility, the disease, and the diagnosis, coding all these things, and checking out the adding. And they were usually pushing you to do six hundred, seven hundred, one thousand, twelve hundred a day. They were incredible. Some people just sat there like machines because they were so intimidated, and wouldn't pick their heads up from their desk from eight in the morning until four-thirty at night.

The people who started the organizing had all blown in in the last two or three years, but we did pick up important support from people who had worked there a long time. One Filipino woman had been working there for quite some time, five or ten years. This union thing really hit her. My floor is way over fifty percent Filipino, and this woman just went out and started hustling these people. There's this big myth that Filipinos are very conservative and don't want to do anything to rock the boat. This woman just talked a lot to the Filipinos there and by the end of the campaign she had us a hundred votes, easy. She not only organized the Filipinos on our floor, but she organized the Filipinos upstairs and downstairs as well. We had to organize along separate lines. We had Filipino organizers, more or less, amongst the Filipino workers, and whites amongst the whites and blacks amongst the blacks. We had leadership in each section.

The Filipinos, about a week before the election, put out a newsletter strictly from the Filipinos' point of view. It talked about the union as a way that the Filipinos could start to solve their problems. It was signed by about twenty or thirty people. When a lot of people sign, it makes it harder to take reprisals.

Most office workers' impression of unions is that they are mostly a bunch of self-serving punks, more interested in their bankrolls than anything else. People just don't trust unions in this country and there are a lot of good historical reasons for that. But as one person at [the company] said, "No matter how bad a union is — I've worked in a lot of places, union and nonunion — and one thing's for sure, the very worst union shop I ever worked in was better than the very best nonunion shop." And that's true — in terms of money, conditions, and everything else. And besides, it's possible to change the union, too.

. . . . . .

In *banking,* few places are unionized, but the number is growing and bank managers themselves are worried. "Banks have become data-handling factories filled with frustrated employees," warned an article in *Bank Administration.* At least twelve banks, including two in New Jersey and one in Washington, D.C., are unionized in the OPEIU. This union also has contracts with banks and insurance companies in Canada. (In other countries, bank unionization is much more widespread than it is in the United States. Bank unionization has been a growing trend in Great Britain and Japan; unionized bank employees in France went out on strike in 1974.) Employees of the New York and American Stock Exchanges, and several Wall Street brokerage firms, have been affiliated with the OPEIU for many years.

Some bank employees (for instance at the First Wisconsin National Bank and the Seattle First National Bank) are organized in their own unions, independent of any larger group. And new unions are starting to organize bank employees. The Steelworkers, for example, represent employees at the United States National Bank in Johnstown, Pennsylvania. The SEIU conducted two major campaigns in California in the spring of 1974 — one at a major credit card company and one at the mighty Bank of America. Employees at Bank of America, the largest commercial bank in the United States, formed an independent association which tried to win recognition from the bank in 1973. That group was defeated by the bank's high-powered antiunion campaign. The following year they were ready to try again. The continuing activity of bank employees, even in

unsuccessful attempts to organize, points to an increasing
trend toward bank unionization.

Margaret was part of the organizing committee in the
credit card company. She describes how that organizing
campaign started, and how she personally got involved:

This guy, a white male, came into our office and he decided he wanted my job. He had no experience at all, but
he came and spoke in front of everybody that he was
tired of working on the machines and he wanted my job.
So my supervisor had me train him, and he was so dumb
that I had to teach him what a debit was and what a
credit was, as if I was teaching my daughter. He could
handle it up to a certain point and then he'd call me
asking what should he do next. After a couple of months
they took me off my job and put me on a machine and
gave him my job. And he was still asking me questions.

Did you file any complaints?

You better believe I did — as fast as I could get to the
office. No one, absolutely no one, does that to me. And
I decided that the only way we could do things was to start
something in the company. This guy had tried to organize
a union in another bank, and we started talking and then
met at his house one day. There were three of us, and we
started thinking about how conditions there were really
right for organizing and that someone should try to
organize that place.

There are, I would say, at least sixty percent Filipino
working there. They get harassed more than anyone. They
have the lowest pay. It's ridiculous. I think many of them
are skilled, but they don't have their citizenship papers.
Also, there are no women in responsible positions. They
have a couple of women in very poor supervisory positions.
They're like "yes" women. Everything is "yes" this, and
"yes" that, "my boss says" this, "my boss says" that. I
went to see one of the women's "bosses" and was complaining about the situation. He told me that if I came
into his office again, he'd can me! This was his answer to
my complaints. This was the grievance procedure.

And there's no chance of promotion there for women,

blacks, or any minorities. It's very seldom a minority gets a good position. [A personnel officer, who] is a white male, said that black people were a pain in the ass.

And the pay is ridiculous!

Were you afraid they'd fire you for organizing?

What if they did? I wasn't making anything anyway! It wouldn't have made that much difference. Anyway, the job is a security crutch. You just struggle to keep this job. You rush and rush and rush and try to keep that job, right? But if you look back and stop, you realize that you're not really getting anyplace. You're working all day and you've done all this, you're scared you might lose that damn job, you come home and clean up, you take care of your kids or your house or whatever you have to do, you take your bath, and you go to bed. And you get up the next morning and you rush again for the same damn job, because you're afraid you're going to be fired if you're not there on time. So you're not really getting anything accomplished. I just refuse to give them all of my life!

The first literature we put out was about the ventilation and the noise and the drafts. I mean, it's really horrible. Sometimes downstairs where I work at, it's so *hot*. Sometimes it's extremely cold because of the air conditioning, and then it will be completely hot. I mean *really* hot. And the turnover's really bad behind that, and sick leave. Lately, I have to say, it's not dirty, but before, it was so dirty there were bugs flying around.

Why did it change?

Everybody started bitching. I think that when the union came in people started feeling a little confident about a lot of things. I even feel now if we ever lose this election, things will never be the same as they were before. I think people are getting confidence — feeling, "They can't push me around anymore!"

6

"It's Possible to
Change the Union,
Too"

Office workers, like others, sometimes find that when they decide to unionize, it's not just the company they have to fight. Unions themselves can present a whole other set of problems.

If they leaf through copies of union newspapers, they will notice that almost all of the pictures of officials show rows of middle-aged white males. Even though women are increasingly active in unions and taking leadership roles at the local level, unions remain male-dominated. Even unions with a large percentage of women members have few women in top leadership or organizing positions. The Office and Professional Employees International Union (OPEIU) has only two women on its thirteen-member Executive Board, despite an approximately seventy-percent female membership. None of that union's international organizers is female. The Service Employees International

Union (SEIU) Executive Board has three female members out of twenty-two. Only two out of nineteen organizers for the American Federation of State, County, and Municipal Employees (AFSCME) New England District are women.

If a clerical group goes to meet with some of these male union officials, they may be treated to pronouncements about how clerical workers and/or women are hopeless and impossible to organize, in spite of growing evidence to the contrary. Or in justifying their own failure to reach more clerical workers, union officials may blame their circumstances — like the OPEIU local leader who said he would be organizing more if he had "a girl" to do the paperwork. Or they may blame the women themselves: "Clerical workers don't care for unions," an AFSCME official explained. An article in the OPEIU newspaper, arguing that people need unions, said, "To union-minded individuals this idea is so simple that they wonder why office women seem unable to grasp it." And some organizers completely miss the boat, like the OPEIU staff member who said, "I haven't given much thought to the women's movement." (This man's *job* is organizing office workers!)

Contempt for women keeps many union officials from trying very hard to organize clerical workers. Some even go so far as to try to *prevent* women from joining their unions. One union official in San Francisco told a union organizer *not* to organize a group of university clericals because he didn't want any more "women's libbers" in the local. (After this advice was ignored and employees organized, the union's national newspaper bragged about it — the "Tenth Institution of Higher Education" to join the union!)

Faced with situations like this, some clerical workers have made the decision to form their own unions, like the group of university clerical workers in British Columbia who have started a province-wide Association of University and College Employees. The AUCE says one reason for going independent is the male domination of existing unions. But organizing an independent union has many drawbacks. Groups who try it, like the Teachers College Employee Association at Columbia University, often find they need the money, legal help, and organizational and

negotiating experience that an established union can provide. Like many others, the Teachers College group decided to affiliate with a larger union after trying independence for a while. Most groups, however, just start out
campaigning for an existing union.

One of the results of the new spirit among women workers is that some unions are beginning to become more
responsive. Several state labor councils — like those in
California, Wisconsin, Arkansas — have held special conferences for union women to get together and discuss common problems. Some unions are active in helping members
fight sex discrimination with legal asistance and educational programs. AFSCME, for example, encourages locals
to start women's rights committees, and publishes information on how to go about it. Some unions also push for anti-
sexist demands in their contracts: for equal job rights, for
maternity leave, and even, in the case of one SEIU contract, for paternity leave.

Perhaps more important, unions like AFSCME in Illinois and SEIU in Boston are beginning to hire more activist women as organizers. As staff members, these women
are in a position to help women employees organize real
grass-roots groups to stand up for their own demands.
Because this, ultimately, is the only way they will succeed.

The group of employees organizing at a California office
of a major credit-card company had their own ideas about
what a union should be. Margaret explains how they had to
start fighting for those ideas as soon as they began their
organizing drive:

There was a lot of doubt when we started because there
were just three persons, and we thought the more persons
the better it would be — which I still think, but it's also
the quality of their thoughts.

We went to one local union and told them what we were
hoping to do — that we would affiliate with them but remain semi-autonomous, that we would be able to write
our bylaws. We wanted to write the literature and make
major decisions. After all, it was our lives, and we figured
that if we can't make our own decisions, why bother! And
they *agreed* to it. This is the amazing thing about it. And

we decided, well, great, we'll be able to use their machinery to write literature. It sounded great.

But what happened is that they felt — this is what we realized later on — that they were professionals and knew more about organizing. They had done it a million times, right? So they knew what we needed more than *we* knew what we needed. I'm not doubting that they might be able to pull a fast one, faster than we could. But we weren't out to pull a fast one. What we wanted to do was organize the workers, *consciously* organize the workers so we can actually struggle *together* — you know, everyone struggling together to get what we want. I think they saw this all as sort of a threat.

Why did you want to join a union if it was like this?

It brings the workers closer. You have to start someplace, and I feel — and I think everyone on the organizing committee feels this also — that if you can get the unity, then you can start working toward a common goal. As long as we just organize one here, one there, we're going to have nothing. If one person gets up, they'll call you a little rebel and they'll just push you out the door. They can easily do this. But I don't think they can do it if we're all united.

Anyway, we set up some meetings and we were passing cards out, underground. The organizer kept making excuses and not showing up at our meetings, so we kept talking to him on the phone — until we found out that he was intending to pass out his own literature the next day, without our consent, without even *telling* us! They pulled out on us after that, but it was just as well because *we* were going to pull out.

Then we decided for a while that we'd try the autonomous thing. I still wonder if that would work, but I wouldn't try it. You're risking too many people's lives, and if it doesn't work, there are a lot of people who are going to be disillusioned. What we did was we went to Union WAGE [Women's Alliance to Gain Equality, a Bay area organization of working women] and talked to them. I think it was a very bad speech we gave, but they were really nice people and seemed to understand. They were willing to help us, you know, leaflet, et cetera, and they

referred us to [another union]. It's working out good as
far as unions are concerned. But really I still have my dis-
illusions about unions.

Are they letting you write your own literature?

Yeah, we're writing it, but we still have problems. We
refused to separate ourselves from the workers. Instead of
saying in our leaflets, *you* should do this or that, we said,
we are going to. There were a couple of pieces of literature
that someone wrote that we scratched out all the "you's"
and put "we's" in. Then we got the literature back from the
union and it was "you's" again. It's this split. The organizing committee was separated from the workers, but we
didn't want it that way. The company keeps saying, "These
outsiders are coming in to rule your life." But almost all
the union literature has said "we," the workers here. So
people are saying, "What outsiders are they talking about?"
So it's working out.

But the organizer has done a lot of things without even
asking us. For instance, he gave the company ninety days
delay for the election in exchange for a list of the workers.
I think it was the worst thing he could have done to the
campaign. We were under the impresion that they were
going to have a hearing on things like this, and we were all
going to be there.

I feel that people should realize that an organizer has a
job. He wants to do his job, that's what he gets paid for. I
feel that a lot of good can come out of his doing his job,
but he has to sometimes be *directed*.

•   •   •   •   •   •

Once a union is voted in, even if the campaign was led
by a strong committee, it's possible for the union to slip
away from being a real organization of workers, and to
become controlled by a few union officials. Vicki, a union
steward, talked about what it's like when that happens:

Our union contract was just negotiated. I was the only
person on the negotiating committee who said that I felt it
was not the best contract we could get and that I wouldn't

recommend voting for it. It was a three-year contract, which is entirely too long. We don't have stable enough working conditions laid out in our contract; we don't have protection enough to go for that long with no changes. The money was another thing foremost in people's minds. The union leadership was constantly saying, "Well, this will fly with the membership," "Well, that's in the ball park, I think we can get them to buy that." That kind of attitude. The membership did buy it — by a sixty-vote margin, out of twelve hundred. That's how many people were angry about it and voted against it, even though you had the union representatives and eleven out of twelve people on the negotiating committee saying, "This is a good contract, vote for it."

What was it like being on the negotiating committee?

Very frustrating. A total farce. The only reason you were there was just for polite role-playing. We had very little serious discussion. It was just a couple of meetings going over the contract and throwing in things we wanted. And then we got to sit around and give it all up. You weren't supposed to talk, you were supposed to pass notes to the business reps.

How does all this affect the day-to-day problems of the membership?

There's a tremendous backup in the grievance process. And, mainly, there is no communication with the membership, and we desperately need it. I can't be an effective steward if people aren't being educated as to their union rights, what the name of the union is, what the grievance procedure is, what is in the contract. A contract negotiated is nothing if you don't use it, and using it is making sure that you have people on every floor who know what the contract is and what their rights are. My idea is that we should have regular meetings of the stewards to deal with the problems of upholding the contract. There are things that we have to do that the union reps can't possibly give us solutions to because they don't work in there. The only solutions we're going to be able to find is by talking with each other. I said I think we should form a stewards' committee and I was attacked; it was subversive.

.   .   .   .

On the basis of her experience in several unions, Carol, an organizer for an industrial union, describes what she sees as the main reasons unions become inactive and undemocratic. She is against the idea that employees should rely on union representatives or "business agents" coming in and talking to employers *for* them (often called "servicing"):

I don't like to use the word "servicing." I have been assigned to cover some servicing, but I won't do it. I go in and teach people how to do it themselves. I don't believe in business agents. I think there should just be resource people employed by the union on an on-call basis, so that if somebody has a legal question, they can get an answer, or if somebody really needs to have the presence of an outside person, they can call.

In contract negotiations, there has to be a negotiating committee, but that can be a very paper thing. Most of us insist that from day one *we* [the outside organizers] don't talk in the negotiations, because that forces the boss to deal with the employees. The day the boss gets used to talking to a union staff person, he doesn't take the employees themselves seriously.

That's something employees can overcome, by simply demanding and insisting that the boss deal directly with them, but the presence of a business agent takes that away from people. They feel that it's an insurance policy — you pay your dues, and that's the premium, and then you have your agent come in and he provides whatever the policy says you're going to have, and that's the contract. It's a concept that everybody has about unions because it's true. It's not *right,* but it's what happens, in large part.

Local union autonomy and self-determination is the whole ball game, particularly for people who are in a small office. If you're my boss and I deal with you on a day-to-day basis, I know the relationship I've established with you

and I don't want any outsider coming in and messing it up.
I may not always like it, but I know you're going to talk
to me and I know I'm going to represent myself. I could
more readily accept approaching the boss with Susie at
the next desk, who may have the same complaint as I do,
than someone flying in from outside and messing it all
up because they're not going to talk to me and they don't
understand.

I think part of the reason for union bureaucracy is a
change in the relationship between the workers and
the management — a change that is probably fostered
by the union. It's the whole idea that you fight the boss
and say what a crumb he is while you're organizing. You
paint this wicked picture, and the people *know* because
they see him and he *is* a crumb, and they don't like him
and there's no reason why they should like him. So you
get them to sign that ballot and then the next day you
walk in and say, "Well, now that we've won the fight,
we'll put our arm on his shoulder and we'll all sit down."
I don't think that negotiations should be conducted in a
friendly atmosphere. I consider that I'm not supposed to be
neutral. I think that the unions neutralize people's feelings
about their boss. That's when organization stops, that's
when people lose interest. It *becomes* an insurance policy.
Somebody else will take care of it. People have other
demands on their time.

But in fact you *can* build your own organization.

.   .   .   .

Members of bureaucratic or inactive unions have sometimes been able to change their unions and restore democracy and membership participation. They have started by
organizing caucuses within the unions. Maxine Jenkins, a
former SEIU organizer, sums up how to get started:

The very first thing to do is to find a friend. From those
two people you can grow into five and six, and develop
into a caucus. The number-one thing is to learn parliamentary procedure backwards and forwards so that you're
not afraid. Have role-playing sessions and consciousness

raising sessions among yourselves. And be as secretive
as the times require.

.   .   .   .   .   .

Kay Eisenhower is a member of a caucus within her
public employees' local. In a California women's newspaper, *Union WAGE,* she wrote about the method of organizing that her group has found successful:

One of the most effective means of organizing a group of
employees to fight for their rights, both on the job and in
the union, is a newsletter. Once the workplace is unionized, there still exists the need for communication between
members and the union they've chosen. If problems
develop between the union leadership and the membership, a newsletter can be a means of carrying on the de-
bate and, if necessary, organizing members to replace
the existing leadership. And finally, the collective experience of putting out a newsletter teaches workers many of
the skills they need to exercise democratic control over
their union structures, and to deal effectively with arbitrary
management actions.

.   .   .   .   .   .

In the late sixties a members' caucus was formed to challenge what they considered an undemocratic and inactive
local leadership in OPEIU Local 29, in Oakland, California. Jean Maddox, a veteran of decades of union activity, helped organize the caucus and was eventually elected
president of the local when the old leadership was defeated:

We started with the idea that we needed a stewards'
council, and that a good steward system would be the best
backbone of the union. Stewards were appointed then by
the union president/senior rep, and if they became militant
and fought for the people in the job, sooner or later management got rid of them and the union didn't fight it.
    Anyway we pressured until we got a stewards' class set
up, and that stimulated the stewards to build a council.
That's how we began. We would meet for dinner just
before union meetings and go over things. Our key issue

was democracy within the local and membership input into decision-making. This was not happening.

In the union meetings we got a lot of "actions" started. We made them hire another business agent. We pushed for a stewards' manual. We had speakers on the health and welfare and pension plans, and speakers on parliamentary procedure and how to handle grievances. One thing we were seeking to do was to divide the responsibility between the president and the senior rep. The then president was also senior rep. After we got a constitutional amendment separating the two jobs, the guy resigned because he knew his goose was cooked.

When it came to negotiations, they would sort of go to the employers saying, "Please, Sir." And then, when they got the best they could that way, they'd come back to the membership and say, "Well, you'd better accept it, that's the best you're going to get." And members, not knowing what else to do, would accept it.

What *we* did when *we* started negotiations was to call proposal meetings of all the people who worked in the place to get all of their input on what they wanted, and then we would type it all up in a letter and send it to the employer. And we *elected* a rank-and-file negotiating committee, where the old president used to *appoint* one, if any. We sort of became known as a striking union there for a while because the employers didn't believe us; they thought they could handle us like they had before. And they found out they couldn't. We had some really fine contracts — not always as a result of strikes, but in the beginning, the first year, we had several strikes. The employers began to recognize that we meant business and then they would settle a better contract *without* a strike.

In 1970 we were negotiating the food-industry contract, which is a master contract [one contract negotiated with many companies in an industry]. To my knowledge it was the first time that a union ever raised the question of discrimination against women in negotiations. There were fourteen other unions in that same business, all male-dominated, and they had all gotten good settlements with no strike. Our union was all women and the employers simply wouldn't talk to us. It was just horrible.

They wanted to take away this and give us a little of that. So right at the negotiating table we began to accuse them of discrimination against women, which blew their minds. Finally we wrote up our offer and they all signed except Lucky Stores. Lucky's wouldn't accept it, so our people went on strike. Clerical people were the ones that were striking, but then every other union in the store, all fourteen of them, observed our picket lines and closed the place down.

Then I got on the phone and called every women's lib group in the area and invited them out on the picket lines, to give us a show of support. It wasn't long before the lib women began to understand the problems of union women and the union women began to see the need to have a liberation movement. It was really great. The women hung in there and they won. And they'll never be the same. They settled their last contract without a strike, because Lucky's knew they meant business.

So we were getting better contracts. We were fighting grievances and going to arbitration; we were beginning to take a few political positions. For example, we were one of the first unions to pass a resolution against the war in Vietnam. And then when the Angela Davis case came up, we passed a resolution supporting her right to bail. That blew the International's mind.

Were you fighting for specifically women's demands?

As far back as 1967 I proposed a maternity leave and the women went for it and we won it. The employers were horrified when we raised it. You could just see it in their eyes. You know — we don't want those unshapely women working in *our* office. It was really hysterical to watch them. So we won that. Women could get their jobs back, no matter what time they left. One thing that we've always had in our contracts is seniority, which does protect women.

We've gotten other clauses in the contract — for example, personal time off, maybe five days a year that you can take in one-hour intervals, so that if a woman wants to take her child to the doctor or whatever, she has that extra time. We've gotten some of our sick-leave

contracts to cover the parent who stays home to take care of a sick child. We've also been successful in getting clauses that sick leave may be used for maternity leave, and we have a health and welfare plan where practically all of maternity benefits are paid for.

If we couldn't win something in the contract negotiations, the union would represent employees and help them file federal suits. And we would represent our people at the unemployment hearings. We never had any equal-pay cases in our local because we have a consistent system that if you do the job, you get the money. It doesn't matter who you are. It also works very well for minority people.

• • • • • • •

After three years of active unionism, Jean's local was put into "trusteeship" by the international union, on charges of election irregularities. This meant that the elected officers were thrown out, the records taken, and membership meetings forbidden. Some union activists feel that this move was just a power play — an attempt by a conservative, male-dominated international leadership to clamp down on an insurgent group. This type of action is not at all rare in unions today, but the OPEIU is considered to be at the conservative end of the union spectrum. There are other internationals that would probably be more tolerant of new leadership and more respectful of local autonomy.

Partly because of the problems they had in unions, some Local 29 people, along with women from other unions in the Bay area, have formed Union WAGE. This group, many of whose members are clerical workers, publishes a newspaper and educational pamphlets, and campaigns for legislation favorable to working women. Its biggest legislative battle concerned protective laws. The group was afraid that the Equal Rights Amendment, if passed, would knock out state laws requiring employers to provide breaks, rest areas, and overtime pay to women. They have campaigned for years to get these benefits extended to men, rather than taken away from women. The group has also been active within the California labor movement, forcing the state AFL-CIO to hold annual conferences for women unionists. Their membership has expanded so rapidly that now they are chartering local Union WAGE chapters in other cities.

One of the strengths of this group is that it includes women of all ages. Although many of its members are young, some of its founders and most active people are older women with many years of union experience. Joyce Maupin started working full time for Union WAGE after being laid off from a clerical job. She describes how the group started and how it helps women in their efforts to organize:

There was a NOW conference in Berkeley on International Women's Day, 1971. A number of trade unionists protested that there was nothing on the program about working women, and as a result a working women's workshop was set up. They decided to have a meeting after the conference to discuss setting up a new organization.

Essentially it was formed to fight for job equality for women and equality within the unions. Women were very underrepresented in unions — about five percent of the leadership and about twenty-three or twenty-four percent of the membership. Besides, those leadership positions were mostly secretary-treasurer. It also tried to nudge the union movement into taking action on women's issues and protective laws, and on organizing. At that point most of us were union members. If we had a big point we wanted to

raise we could bring a simultaneous motion to about
twenty union membership meetings. We did it around
protective laws and the minimum wage and sometimes
other issues.

So, from the beginning there was an idea that this was
an organization that would help women to function within
their unions. To begin with, most women don't know
how to function in a union. They don't know anything
about parliamentary procedure, which is very important
or you just get ruled out of order as soon as you open
your mouth. And you need to know your own shop contract — most women that I knew had never read it. You
need to read your union constitution and see all the
various points and bylaws and traps and everything.

In addition to lack of knowledge, most women are a
little hesitant to speak up, especially since the meetings are
usually chaired by men who are pretty sarcastic and
call people out of order pretty easily. Over the years at
many membership meetings, someone has given a talk on
some aspect of these problems. It's very important to give
people experience in speaking and talking on a point
in a supportive atmosphere.

Do you think you have affected the unions?

There's no doubt about it. They were never conscious
of any sort of women's problems in the unions before we
came along and they were forced to think about them.

*How can a group which is not itself a union help organize
unorganized women?*

If the unions were functioning well, we wouldn't be
needed. But women have become so distrustful of unions
that they hesitate to go directly to the union, and/or if
they do, they may get such an unpleasant reception that
they're completely turned off. And then they sort of hear
that there's a working women's organization around that
knows a lot about unions and they call us up.

This happened with the Earring House workers. They
had gone to one union and they said they felt as though
they were being interviewed by an employer, not by somebody who was supposed to be organizing them. Then

they called Union WAGE and I set up a meeting with them where we discussed what unions are like, how they function, and that they should insist on their own rank-and-file committee if they join a union, and not let anybody take it over and so forth, which is what they wanted anyway.

In other cases, members of Union WAGE try to organize the places where they work. In the Bank of America campaign, Union WAGE members go to the organizing meetings and make suggestions about flyers and organizing techniques and plans. [During one recent clerical campaign,] Union WAGE members or friends did all the leafletting. They didn't want anybody at [the company] to stick their necks out. And don't think *that* wasn't a hard assignment, because one of the time slots was quarter to six in the morning! They'd go down before they went to work and leaflet.

And we get letters sometimes from women in various parts of the country who are having problems with their unions, or just organizing problems. "How do I organize secretaries in North Carolina?" Sometimes I say, "Well, you can start your own union. You call it an association. You get a bunch of people together and get them to sign cards. A lot of unions are started that way. And it's just as legal as any established union; it's just kind of hard."

One of the funnier letters said, "Tell us a good non-sexist union to join." I did write back, "There is no such thing. You have to get in there and fight."

7

Up Against

Mahogany Row

When office workers begin to protest and organize, few employers sit idly by. Even the smallest sign of rebellion is likely to produce a flood of management countermeasures, from nice chats to ridicule, from free lunches to harassment, from new privileges to sudden firings. Employee actions on a larger scale, like union-organizing, are met with the big guns: professional anti-labor lawyers and well-orchestrated public relations campaigns using literature, employee meetings, and subtle threats.

Management consulting firms and businessmen's organizations pour money and expertise into research on how to prevent employees from organizing and to defeat union drives if they occur. Executives attend conferences and workshops on how to prevent organizing within their companies. They have access to published reports with titles like "White Collar Restiveness: A Growing Challenge" [1] and "How to Meet the Problem of White Collar Organizing." [2]

Why do employers put so much effort into stopping employees from organizing? It's partly money. All the management theories about preventing employee organization tell bosses they *must* provide decent pay and benefits. Otherwise they're asking for it. But somehow, it still works out that when the boss alone decides how much to pay, it's usually less than what would result from a negotiation. A Labor Department study in the late sixties found that among non-office workers, unionized employees got paid an average of $1.29 an hour more than people not in unions. [3]

Still, some non-union companies pay a little *above* the average, just to keep unions out. Why is it worth it to them? One lawyer who specializes in helping companies defeat union-organizing campaigns explained it like this: The value of remaining non-union, he said, was that as a boss you "retain the right to make unilateral day-to-day business judgments," which was a "very important right." [4]

That sounds reasonable, until you stop and think about what some of those business judgments could be: See how little she'll accept as a starting salary. Lay off twenty in accounting. Bring in that new machine and assign her to work on it full time. Skip the training, it's too expensive. Don't bother to hire another girl; just divide up the work among the ones left. Anyone late three times in a month will be suspended.

Most managers don't want employees meddling in these decisions. Employees' desires for a voice in the policies that affect them are a direct threat to this unilateral control. So when office workers start to organize, stopping them is serious business for their employers.

Even before the slightest sign of "trouble," alert employers are preparing for that possibility. At the 1973 personnel conference of the American Bankers Association, experts warned bank executives to think ahead. "With most banks currently non-union," they were told, "now is the best time to establish and maintain permanent standing committees to plan for any eventual union-organizing drives." [5] The first step in preventing unionization is to ward it off with a variety of tactics for "winning the hearts and minds" of employees — manipulating them into feeling that they can't or shouldn't organize. Many of these tactics can be identified.

1. THE MODERN OFFICE

One of the current fads in the employee morale business is office furniture and decor: offices with brightly colored partitions instead of straight wood and glass; decorating in yellow and orange to make employees feel "up"; wall-to-wall carpeting, for a feeling of luxury.

Office furniture companies sell their products on the basis of what they can do for morale. One ad about word-processing centers reads, "Someone else has solved the machinery problems. Herman Miller is now able to say we can solve your people problems . . . [Herman Miller office furniture] gives the people in your office a very personal and efficient place to work. And it gives them something as all-important as dignity. Humanity in an age of machines." [6]

During a tour of one Boston bank, it was proudly pointed out that it had "upgraded" its word-processing center — new furniture, new machines. Have the salaries been raised in this "upgrading?" Well, no. But the bank also allows people to drink coffee at their desks, and has a special little lounge for one of its downtown typing pools. Bright colors and carpeting and informality are supposed to "solve the people problems" by providing a sense of humanity and dignity. Maybe they hope employees will be so pleased with the surroundings that they won't protest highly pressured, routine, and low-paid work.

2. THE LITTLE EXTRAS

Big clerical employers with a non-union tradition often provide other little extras — like subsidized cafeterias, company-run clinics and training courses (although clerical workers are often barred from classes because the subject is not related to their particular jobs). Upon closer examination, you see that many of management's little treats don't cost the company anything. One Boston bank, for example, offers low car-insurance rates. They don't pay for the insurance, but they can arrange for a low rate because of the size of the group. Many insurance companies run discount gift, card, and record shops, and boast employee "clubs" which sponsor trips and buy discount tickets to sports events.

The psychology behind these little extras is not just that people will like them; all together, they are supposed to give people the feeling that this is an *impressive* place to work, something big and exciting to be part of. Universities and publishing houses have another version of this strategy. They try to convince employees that it's a privilege to be able to work for this distinguished intellectual institution — a privilege that is much more important than a little thing like money.

The real payoff for the employer comes when someone mentions "union." If an employer's tactics have been effective, the employees will react as one group of secretaries did: "Well, when we all go out, they pay for our lunch, they give us a Christmas bonus, they send us off to a work-

shop. You know, they do little things throughout the year
... Right now, this is basically a really good office to
work in." Meanwhile their employers have maintained
their right to make unilateral judgments — including the
possibility of stopping the little extras any time.

3. COMMUNICATION

Enlightened companies are also advised by personnel experts to establish written policies to make employees feel
they are being dealt with fairly — "according to the rules"
— so they won't feel the need for the protection of an organized employee group. The company should make employees think that they are being listened to by establish-
ing an employee-complaint "hotline" or suggestion system.
One management text said that in the DuPont company
"a special effort is made to encourage every person to come
through with one suggestion that can be accepted. They
feel that this will make a 'believer' of him [sic] for life." [7]

Management training today stresses *motivating* employees, rather than just ordering them around. Giving the
worker a sense of involvement. Some even set up student-
council-type employee organizations, which get to decide weighty matters like what kind of food to have for the
Christmas party. Also imitating high school, one anti-union
expert urged managers to turn the official company newspaper over to employees, so they wouldn't be as likely to
start a protest newsletter.[8]

The catch is the unilateral judgments. After all of the
formal procedures and communications, it's still the boss
who decides. And all the participation may just end up like
the individually controlled thermostats rumored to be in
Boston's old John Hancock building. You could adjust
your own thermostat, all right — but it wasn't hooked up
to anything.

4. THE SELF-IMPROVEMENT GAME

Traditionally, secretaries also were manipulated with
advice about being cheerful, subordinate, supportive, and

hard-working. It may seem that this type of advice went out with white gloves, but today it just takes the form of psychological insight and tips on how to get ahead.

One example of this tactic is a traveling workshop called "Management Education for Secretaries," to which companies can send secretaries for the day. In a plush hotel conference room, the secretaries hear a lecturer explain that the session will help them identify with their bosses' roles. Their goal as secretaries should be the success of their boss. They are told how they can improve themselves, their attitudes, and work habits in order to get more done and be more helpful to the boss. Doing extra work, the lecturer says, should be welcomed as a chance for personal growth. You shouldn't expect more money *too*. You are already getting "psychic wages" — personal satisfaction from learning on the job. (For men, responsibility and creative work are justifications for big paychecks. But for women office workers, interesting work is supposed to be a *substitute* for a good salary.) A professional, the secretaries are told, is self-motivating. "You don't need the carrot of next year's contract with more money." [9]

This is just a modern version of the old-fashioned philosophy of "blame yourself." It's especially effective on women. We've all been taught to try frantically to improve our imperfect selves — hair, clothes, weight, personality, work habits. But isn't this convenient for the employer? If this strategy succeeds, the secretaries will work harder and harder, not asking for any more money in return, convinced that they are contributing to their own self-improvement. And the boss gets to keep all the carrots for himself.

5. DIVIDE AND CONQUER

Favoritism and "office politics" also serve to distract employees from challenging employers' policies, as well as to make it harder to organize. A clerk's newsletter describes how this works: "Many supervisors feel that promoting a certain amount of disunity is necessary to maintain control in an office. Their strategy is simple — favoritism. For example, in one office where transfers occurred, experienced women with good records were passed over in favor of a relatively inexperienced person. The promoted person is an able worker, but the lack of consideration of seniority created very bad feelings. The favorites in the office have been promised upgradings and better work assignments. Those who are less favored are given less desirable assignments and rarely receive any praise for good work. These differences in treatment, in turn, have resulted in strained work relationships and there has been a lot of backbiting and discord." [10]

Sometimes favoritism is complicated by other factors. When the favored and the less favored belong to different races or sexes or age groups this pattern can get even worse. Another variation is the aspiring Don Juan, who flirts with a favored few and, if he's successful, stirs up rivalry and jealousy in the office.

Sophisticated office managers use favoritism to siphon off people who might lead protests, and get them on the company's side. One text advises bosses to spot these informal leaders, "keeping them well informed, consulting them frequently in making decisions which influence employee interests, and observing them as prospects for promotion." [11]

A city hospital clerk described an incident which shows how favoritism can be used to prevent workers from organizing. In her hospital a supervisor promoted a young, inexperienced man over the heads of many women with years of work in the department. A common story — but this time the women got together and went in a group to demand that he give the promotion to one of them instead.

While this conflict was going on, the boss hinted to one of the women involved that she might be in line for a pay increase. Her friend, who was doing exactly the same work, was furious at being left out. The two women started arguing, and soon the whole office was drawn into taking sides. People stopped speaking to each other, and the tension grew. In this case the union steward was able to call a meeting where the people worked it out. But as long as the office was divided by this quarrel, their boss was free from complaints about his sexist promotion policies.

In spite of all these managerial efforts, office workers *are* starting to protest against injustices on the job. When someone in an office starts talking back to the boss or trying to organize a group of employees to discuss job problems, she or he may find the boss's attitude change. Although some supervisors take it in stride or are genuinely sympathetic, more often the response is ridicule, harassment, or hostility. To the employee just beginning to protest, these reactions can seem very personal. But they are also tactics — part of a larger management effort to retain that unilateral control. They are successful when they can scare other people in the office away from becoming active or trying to change things.

A "9 to 5" activist describes how this works in her office: "One woman said to me, 'Why should I get involved? They all walk by you and say, "Hey, you women's libber, you want to get me my coffee today?" I don't want to have to put up with that.' Some bosses will bring people into their office and say, 'Have I done something wrong? Why don't you come in and tell me?' "

One Women Employed member got the full treatment from the attorneys in her law office after she organized secretaries to request more vacation time and on-the-job legal training:

We drafted a memo about legal training for secretaries and put a copy on each of the partners' desks. There was such an uproar I'll never forget it. One of the attorneys said we were power-hungry women and we should be chained to our typewriters. We were just trying to show that we were willing to take on extra responsibility! Then we posted the Secretaries' Bill of Rights in the kitchen. The attorneys guffawed over it for thirty minutes and the next day called a meeting.

The lawyers began a divide-and-conquer tactic. They started very subtle intimidation — like rumors that "There's going to be some heads rolling." So right away the secretaries said, "Wait a minute. We're going to lose our jobs." Sides would start forming. They knew I was a leader, so they wanted to get rid of me.

All the secretaries knew I was being watched. The

attorneys were telling me I was late, saying, "This is your last warning." I started showing up a half hour early every day, so they couldn't get me there. Then they were watching my lunch hours, so I was very careful about that. Then they started with, "You have a very bad attitude, very uncooperative." My boss complained because I didn't sharpen his pencils, and his associate complained because I didn't clean off his desk. It got very petty because they couldn't get me on anything really solid. They knew, and I knew, that my work was really good.

I had always thought that my boss was a very fair person and something of a humanitarian until this started. Then I realized that all he was interested in was money, and that the issues involved were going to cost him money because he was going to have to give his secretaries better raises and benefits.

When nothing else worked, they assigned me to a new associate. At first we got along very well — till I realized he was something of a double agent. He would tell me, "This WE business is really terrific. Tell me everything you're doing." So I was stupid and told him. So he went back and told management everything.

The whole experience was very stressful. It was just incredible, it was such a heavy atmosphere. There were other secretaries involved, but they got intimidated, so they dropped out when they saw what I was going through. It got to the point where they would look over their shoulder to see who was around before they came to talk to me. If we had all stuck together, there's no way they could have singled out one person.

But the more pressure they put on me to quit, the more determined I became to succeed. I realized the only way I could succeed would be to unite all the legal secretaries, and go back into that office someday with a bargaining agent for secretaries. I am firmly convinced that's going to happen.

·   ·   ·   ·   ·   ·   ·

Not all organizing efforts are met with the kind of all-out psychological warfare this WE member encountered. The more solidly united employees are, the harder it is for management to create this kind of intimidating atmosphere, and the easier it is for employees to resist whatever pressure is put on them. Some companies, however, go even further, and actually fire people they see as "troublemakers."

Firing or even harassing employees for trying to organize is illegal. The National Labor Relations Act protects the right of employees to organize, not only in unions, but in any type of group, formal or informal, that aims to improve salaries or working conditions. The law says that employers may not influence employees' organizing efforts with violence, firings, spying, intimidation or discrimination, promises or bribes.

Employers, in fact, break this law all the time. They send "loyal" employees to report on organizing meetings. They raise salaries during union organizing efforts. But probably the most common violation is firing someone for organizing. Harold Kowal of the National Labor Relations Board estimates that twenty thousand complaints about these firings are filed each year.[12] He points out that each of the people fired has a group of co-workers who are probably intimidated by the firing — maybe an average of fifty people. So that's one million people each year who get the message that they don't *really* have the right to organize.

Of course the National Labor Relations Board (the agency that enforces the National Labor Relations Act) gets some of these people rehired, and wins cash settlements for even more of them. In many cases the law does really work to protect people, even if they aren't members of an established union. A Boston University secretary got a cash settlement after she was fired for organizing an employee protest committee.[13] And a Pennsylvania bank teller was reinstated and awarded back pay after her firing.[14] Her offense had been complaining, together with other employees, about a bank policy that required them to eat lunch near their teller windows, and jump up and wait on customers if they appeared.

But many times employers do get away with firing people who organize, especially since employees don't always know their rights. This is even more true in clerical occupations, since so few people have union experience.

While the law may not always help employees, it *has* helped the legal profession by creating a whole new occupation — the "anti-labor" lawyer, the person who gives companies legal advice in dealing with unions. Lawyers with this specialty were used in over eighty percent of the white-collar organizing campaigns studied in one survey.[15] Much of their advice concentrates on how to violate the *spirit* of labor law without doing anything technically illegal.

They are good at the subtleties. When is a threat not a threat? When it's a statement of "fact or opinion." Yale, for example, hired anti-union experts to defeat a clerical organizing drive.[16] They told employees, among other things, that there was "no guarantee that present benefits would continue" [17] if the union was voted in. Threatening to withdraw these benefits is illegal. But this was just a statement of fact.

Spying on employees, or trying to find out what they think about unions, is illegal. But it is legal, and strongly advised by anti-labor experts, for a manager to have small group meetings, or even one-to-one chats with employees about the union. He should not ask what the employees' views are. But if they volunteer information, it's not his fault. (A pamphlet on how to deal with "white collar restiveness" suggests more insidious ways of finding out what employees are thinking. It says that a counseling service is a good way to "sense changes in individual or group attitudes," and points out that "doctors and nurses constitute an unusually good source of information about the ebb and flow of dissatisfaction." [18])

Firings are, of course, legal, even during a union organizing campaign, *if* they're for a good cause unconnected with organizing. And if an employee has been vocal in protest, management may look very hard for a good cause. During a recent union drive in a New Haven bank, one of the activists violated a rule that seemed to be commonly violated by all the bank employees. But management was watching him, so out he went. One pamphlet for white-collar employers provides a three-page list of all the reasons that the NLRB had ruled permissible grounds for firing someone during a union drive.[19]

Labor laws can be avoided. But they can also be *used* by employers with good legal advice. "Delay," said Kowal of the NLRB, "The employers play it like you play a harp." [20] A common way is a battle over "unit determination" — who should be included in the group to vote on the union. A classic example was the effort of one stock-brokerage firm to challenge the New York "unit" in which the Office and Professional Employees Union was organizing. The company wanted to have just one election for all of their employees on the East coast, from North Carolina to Maine.[21] If they had won the case, the group would have been so large it would have been very difficult to organize. But even in losing they had delayed the union election for months.

Lawyers who help with these tactics are only one resource managers use. There are a number of management consulting groups that hold seminars and workshops on how to defeat unions, like the one given for the American Bankers' Association.[22] A new group which also seems to concentrate on white-collar unionization is the National Center for the Study of Collective Bargaining in Higher Education. The Bureau of National Affairs holds annual conferences on collective bargaining for employers in various locations around the country. That group also publishes a weekly bulletin called *White Collar Report*, which describes current employee organizing activity. In addition, local management organizations sponsor meetings on "How to Maintain Non-Union Status" and "Staying Union-Free."

Other groups publish occasional studies of white-collar organizing and how to defeat it. The most recent was a study called *White Collar Unionization*, put out in 1970 by the National Industrial Conference Board. This group sent a questionnaire to 140 companies where white-collar union elections had recently been held. They made a statistical analysis of the factors that made union success more likely — presumably so the reader could figure out how to avoid it. They included quotes from managers on the secrets of their successes in defeating unions, and pages of quotes from company anti-union propaganda. In case the employer-reader still couldn't figure out a strategy, the report included a case study of a company's success (the union lost two to one), with details from management's anti-union campaign.[23]

That model company reported, among other things, that it held *daily* meetings with supervisors during the union campaign. Stressing the importance of supervisors to an anti-union campaign, one lawyer advised special efforts by top management to make first-line supervisors feel like part of the management team — holding dinners for them, giving them little things to decide. Then when a union drive does develop, he said, you can call them together and say, "You are part of management, and if it's the company policy to defeat the union we have the right to expect you to be part of that effort." [24] Nothing in the labor law protects supervisors who might be accused of not giving their all to the team.

Armed with expensive lawyers and expert advice, managements meet union organizing campaigns with lively countercampaigns. A typical management effort includes a series of letters mailed to employees' homes, leaflets handed out at work, personal chats, meetings on company time, and visual displays. (One manufacturing company went so far as to have its anti-union slogans done up in fine steel lettering.)

John, an organizer and employee in a West Coast office of a major insurance company, had the opportunity to observe elaborate anti-union tactics, from the receiving end:

On my floor I was sort of a leader. So my supervisor started really getting on my case. She's supposed to check the work of ten people. For several months she seemed to spend her entire eight-hour day checking my work. She would pick through every single little jot and cross-T I did. She corrected the way I did my nine's. That was a really big one.

People used to be able to bring coffee to their desks. One day I brought coffee up to my desk and they had a big floor meeting to announce that from then on, nobody could bring coffee up to their desk. You've really got to develop a psychological shield. The company's idea is to harass you until they force you to quit.

My supervisor used to take me aside and try to convince me that I was neurotic. She'd go, "I see you're late again today." "No I'm not, I'm on time." "Well, I see you were *almost* late." "Well, I guess I was almost late, so what does that mean?" "Well you were late and almost late a lot of days this month. How long have you had this problem?" And she'd go on, "Are you sure you're really cut out for working?" "Well, what else am I cut out for, starving?"

It was just sickening. You develop a barrier in your head like — okay, I know these people are really crazy or semi-crazy, and I'm not going to let crazy or semi-crazy people get to me and mess my life up. And if we can organize this place, we will in some way have struck back. I think that for me this was sort of the key that I really got my mind set to after a while. I know that we've got this campaign and if this campaign succeeds, they will not be able to mess with me. So that's how you keep on top of it — by thinking that you're going to win, and looking forward to what you're going to get if you succeed. Don't dwell on the hassles you're having now.

Did you hear about the gala dinner?

How soon before the union election was it?

A week or ten days, something like that. All of the workers and all of the top managers were there. One of them — he was really a trip. He looked like he came out of central casting for corporate executive — very distinguished. He was going around hugging people and putting his arm around these Grade B and Grade C file clerks, and sitting at tables with them. It was just ridiculous. The whole thing of course was to sort of take the edge off the alienation that had developed in the company, which was one of the reasons that the union had been able to get such a foothold. They served us this big dinner.

Then there was an anti-union committee, which was nine-tenths management. I forget what they called themselves. They were just the most sickening people and nobody liked them. It really didn't have much effect. They were secretaries of higher-ups, mostly.

They also gave us a dental plan right before the deadline

for filing the petition, which was sort of a buy. But it was a lousy dental plan, it turned out.

They had captive audience meetings, which means that they take you group by group off your floor. And you go upstairs into the big carpeted office in soft chairs and people are wearing ties and nylons. And then they say, "Now, we want to talk to you about the union. Do you have any questions? We'd like to answer them, ... blah-blah." Of course nobody says anything, and they launch into a ridiculous tirade about how you won't be able to flush the toilet without asking the union; the union's just going to completely run your life; before we could always just *talk* about these things, but *now* ... They'd use every routine they could think of. They used the sweet talk and the get-tough talk.

Captive audience meetings, if they're done right, can be just murder on an organizing campaign. You can have as many meetings as you like. They used to be illegal but now they are legal. Just bring the people in there and have a real sharp-talking lawyer who will totally intimidate anybody that tries to ask a question or cross-examine his statements. Then spread a variety of fifty outright lies, fifty falsehoods, fifty half-truths, fifty questionable truths and just a kind of potpourri of misinformation mixed in with enough information to just really confuse the hell out of people. You sort of scatter about fifty possible doubts that people could have about unions. And the union can't be represented there either. And the union, of course, can't have captive-audience meetings. If they spread fifty doubts, and the union in some way or another is able to deal with three of them, that's forty-seven of them that are untouched and festering in people's heads. That's what the company did, but they didn't do it well. We won!

•   •   •   •   •

Katherine, a member of an organizing committee for a union at a major New York publishing house, witnessed similar tactics:

An organizing committee wrote a letter to management stating that we had an organizing drive and that our right to do so was protected by law. Once you sign such a letter, presumably the employer has to show really good cause for firing you. But you still take a risk.

Management began having these meetings to sort of brief its supervisors about what was bad about the union and what they should tell their employees — how you would have to punch a time clock, how unions could make you go out on strike, how they could tell you what to do, how it would hold you back, stuff like that. They have an industrial relations man on staff who was called in and held these briefing sessions. Very few supervisors fell for it. Also, not long after the organizing drive got under way, all of the eight lowest grades of jobs got an across-the-board eight percent raise.

Another thing the company did was hire a black woman, which is a traditional way of killing two birds with one stone, to head up the affirmative action plan. She instituted something called the direct line, and on special blue stationery, with an envelope marked confidential, you could write out your complaint and send it to her and she would then schedule an appointment with you. Totally confidential. And she would work out your problem with you, whatever it was. Of course, everybody thought she reported right to management. People who were naive enough to go to her with a problem would be told by their supervisors that they had a bad attitude.

Anyway, the women's group had its first open meeting on a Wednesday night. On Friday the union filed for an election. Also on Friday this vague memo from management went up on all the bulletin boards, threatening general layoffs due to the economic situation.

Monday the whole place was in chaos, work ground to a halt. What point was there in doing your work if you were going to get fired the next day? They began calling people up in groups to fire them. Everyone sat around, keeping a tally on who had been fired, and waiting for the phone call. And when the word had come through that someone else had been fired, it would spread like wildfire. People were angry and outraged.

By Tuesday, close to two hundred people had been fired in the space of two days. Several people had resigned

in protest. The firings made no sense in terms of which
departments were profitable and which were not. They
were the heaviest on the floors where the most organizing
had been taking place. The company was very careful
not to fire only union activists or women's group people.
They sort of swept everybody into this general sweeping
out. But they got rid of enough key people or active
people to frighten the rest, cut the heart out of the organizing. That is why we filed an unfair labor charge with
the Labor Board — to try to show that this was a retalia-
tory measure and that it came on the heels of an organizing drive.

·   ·   ·   ·   ·   ·   ·

There's something fundamentally dishonest about all the
company arguments against organizing. Managers give employees lots of good reasons not to vote for the union, but
they never give their *real* reasons for wanting to keep the
union out. They never talk about their very important right
to make unilateral judgments, or the fact that pay is lower,
on the average, in non-union companies.

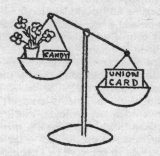

Instead they sound very concerned for the employees'
welfare. They talk about the union as an outside force, in
spite of the fact that employees initiate most organizing
campaigns. The union is portrayed as a large, powerful
organization that wants to tell you what to do and make
money off you (as opposed to, say, the company!!). They
constantly talk about the union ordering people out on

strike, in spite of the fact that even the most bureaucratic unions have to have membership votes on whether to strike — *and* in spite of the fact that the vast majority of union contracts are signed without strikes.

To these standard anti-union arguments, white-collar employers often add two more. With rhetoric about "regimentation" and "individual bargaining," they try to appeal to people's feelings that "If I'm just *good* enough, I'll be rewarded for my individual merit." Maybe. But that's up to the boss's "unilateral judgment." And for everybody who wins that game, many more lose. The other special pitch for offices is snob appeal. Unions are for *factory* workers. That feeling — "I'm just not the type of person who protests" — is part of the reason why office workers are so low-paid and powerless today. In the words of a union button made by Harvard employees, "You can't eat prestige."

The amount and variety and ingenuity of all these efforts show something about employers' feelings toward clerical unions. They are very serious about maintaining their freedom to make "unilateral business judgments" without having to allow employees any say. They obviously have money and expertise and organization far beyond what is available to the people who work in their offices. They obviously can hurt people who start to organize — they have done it and will do it again.

And yet office workers are organizing — and winning victories. Why do they take the risks of standing up to this barrage from mahogany row? The basic reason is that management's unilateral judgments have left office workers low-paid, without adequate benefits, and subject to rigid rules and degrading treatment. Besides, many workers object to their powerlessness on the job — the very thing that management is trying to preserve by keeping employees unorganized.

8

"You <u>Can</u> Build

Your Own

Organization"

If you look around a typical office at three o'clock some Tuesday afternoon, you have a sense of placid order — the fluorescent lights hum, typewriters clack, work is being ground out under the watchful eyes of supervisors, coffee cups are filled. People are thinking about work, or how many hours are left, or personal problems. It's hard to imagine it all turning into a scene of protest and confrontation. A dissatisfied office worker sitting at one of these desks may well wonder *how* people in offices like this are able to organize.

Anyone with organizing experience has made hundreds of mistakes and learned hundreds of lessons. There's no secret formula that can be explained in a few pages. The best way to learn how to go about organizing is to talk, either in formal classes or informal discussions, with people who have this experience and are sympathetic to your goals.

Many colleges and universities have labor-education programs. Some of these are run by professors or union bureaucrats who teach contempt for the membership. Others are run by sincere people with a goldmine of experience. NOW chapters and other women's groups may also have valuable organizing experience to share. And there is a school of organizing called the Midwest Academy that is closely associated with Women Employed and provides courses on organizing techniques and strategies.

But there *are* some basic pointers that can be put down on paper. While not complete enough to be in any way a guide to organizing, the following comments of organizers offer some insight into how office workers have gone about starting and building groups, confronting employers, and resisting the repression they encounter.

I. GETTING TOGETHER

Karen Nussbaum (organizer, "9 to 5"): The first thing people say to me is *"Nothing* ever happens around here because *nobody* ever wants to do anything. I'm the only person who *cares.* How can I do anything? I'm all alone."

Now, that's a defense. I mean, it's hard to think of what to do, for one thing. And it's also true that people *are* "apathetic," but that apathy comes from real sources. The sources are fear of losing your job and cynicism about change. People haven't seen people effectively work to change things. The steps for moving from a gripe to a solution aren't clear to them. You have to move from feeling that you are all alone to recognizing that your gripes are common ones and that you can also *act* on the gripe by building a group.

What I do is try to help people go the first step and get an idea for the second step. To realize that if you come up against what seems to be a brick wall, there's a way to get around it. There aren't unsolvable problems. They don't exist!

What we suggest to people is, if you feel that you're the only person who feels the way you do, first of all, write up a list of every complaint you have about where you work. *Everything.* From the arrangement of desks to the pay. Anything you can think of. The fact that you couldn't get a blotter the other day because the red tape was so thick, or that you don't know what the health plan is, or you don't know what the salary-review procedure is, since it's kept confidential. Or that raises come out in July but they get set in December and you don't ever know what they are. Make as extensive a list as you can. Then make another list of all the people who work in your department, your office or your building, and count them. Just see exactly who's there. And then begin to think, well, what do these people think about these different issues? And then talk to those people about those problems, and before you know it, you've got a group of people that's concerned about a similar set of issues. And then the group has to decide to take some action. That can be as simple as writing a memo that highlights several of those problems, ranging from hard-to-get to easy-to-get. And then take it from there.

Day Creamer (organizer, Women Employed): We talk a lot in Women Employed about the difference between being the office crusader and the office organizer. The office crusader is the person that always has to be out in front, pushing the other people, saying, "This is what we have to do" — which most of the time will turn the other people in the office off. It just won't work. The responsibility of somebody who works in an office and wants to change things is to *care* about the people they're working with and to discuss issues *with* them. And let the militancy of the group evolve.

Carol (organizer for an industrial union, describing the union campaign she helped lead when a secretary at a large state university): The easiest way to start is by taking your original group of organizers, even if it's two people, and going through a whole list of employees, which you can generally intercept from somebody who is clerical. Or start putting together a list yourself. Who do you know that works in the Food Science Department up on the third floor? Well, I know so and so, and so and so. You have to do it first by contacting people that you know, even though you may not know what their reception is going to be.

We visited people where they were eating lunch, visited people in their break areas. We tried some social things, like coffee hours. We would buy coffee and pastry and bring it into the break area. And rather than make a speech, it would just be an opportunity. You know, they say, "Who brought the coffee?" and that gets the conversation started.

We tried to make our literature address real problems that people had expressed to us, rather than use some kind of a stock leaflet about why they needed the union. We went around getting people to talk to us in these little coffee meetings about incidents — of speedup, or added duties, or no promotions.

One of the big things was that nobody on the campus had ever been paid overtime for office work, and the state law clearly says that state employees shall receive overtime pay after a certain number of hours and that compensatory time off is illegal. Some of the office workers liked "comp" time, until you pointed out to them how much money they were losing. That's something everybody could respond to because there probably wasn't a person who wasn't working overtime on the campus. We got a whole bunch of the forms you had to use to request overtime pay, and just gave them to everybody. So the secretaries filled out the form — I worked so many hours, this is the pay I should get — and took it to their department head to sign. He said, "What's this?" and they said, "This is an official state document. It says so right on the bottom, and here's a copy of the law for you to refer to."

That started some money coming in to people. We put out a leaflet right after that about "Can you afford paying *non*-union dues? The non-union dues you've been paying is all this money that you lost over the last twenty years because you didn't have any overtime." Then people started wondering what other things would happen when we had a union.

Ramon Castellblanch (organizing-committee member, at a major insurance company): When you want to organize, the main thing is that you have to talk people into joining the union. Talking people into anything is a one-on-one, very personal process. You can't just stand one hundred people in a room and talk them all into something at once. You've got to go and sit down with each person, individually, and find out what their dad said about unions, what union their grandfather was in, what city they're from and all this other stuff, and put it together. Find out whatever personal objections they might have — "Well, I hear that with unions you might have to punch in on a time clock and that's just awful to me. I'd rather make two hundred dollars a month less than to have to punch in on a time clock." You have to find out where people are coming from and then explain on a one-to-one level — relate unionism to them so that they make a personal decision that they are going to vote for the union. That's how our union elections were won.

Margie Albert (organizer, Distributive Workers of America, District 65, former legal secretary): You can start by setting up an employee association or a women's committee. Companies will often sanction a women's committee. They don't think it's going to be trouble and they'll let you meet on the premises sometimes. Then you can start talking to people about what the issues are.

If you've got a small group together, you can begin shopping around for a union. Go and ask them certain questions. Ask to see some of their contracts. Ask questions to find out how democratic they are, who makes the decisions, who's going to decide on the contract demands. Do you get to ratify your contract? Do you get a secret ballot vote before you go on strike?

Our organizing is done inside an office for the most part, not by "professional" organizers outside. We try to convince the first people who come to us that they have to try to identify what will be in the self-interest of the rest of the people. If you have an office that has middle-aged women and young women, and the young women come to the union because they want maternity leave, you're also going to have to find some issue that appeals to those older women, because they're no longer planning on having babies. And so you talk pensions, or wages, or whatever it is, to bring the two groups together.

Maxine Jenkins (former organizer, Service Employees International Union, Local 400, San Francisco): Clerical workers are so isolated and separated from each other by cubicles, by offices, by buildings, floors, and so forth that you've got to have something to bring them together to overcome this feeling of isolation. So we had a newsletter called the *Clerks' Scoop,* which is one of the basic tools of organizing clerical workers. All the articles were written by the women clerical workers.

The biggest problem in organizing women workers, I find, is that their dual responsibility in the home prevents them from being as active in attending meetings as men. And that's why you have to shape your meetings around the time that women have free — lunchtime, coffee time, and immediately after work.

I would go in and have buffet luncheons or coffee klatches and things like that and say, "Look what your wages are. There's no reason why your wages have to be this way, because unionized office workers make thirty percent more." And then I would always talk about how important clerical work is, and how difficult and skilled it is, and how that is not recognized. Everybody knows that businesses and offices are run by clerks.

And I would point things out like this, and people would smile. I would say, "You have all these skills, and your wages are so low. Can anybody think of why this is so?" And a hand would go up, and somebody would say, "It's because most of us are women."

I believe that you do need female organizers to organize women workers. You can have an organizing staff that has men on it, but you've got to have some female representation. There is great distrust on the part of women for male union organizers. There's a lot of reason behind that distrust. Male organizers will often go out and organize on the basis of their sex appeal. And they will also relate to women as sex objects. They have a fine rapport with the young women, perhaps based on some sexual relationship, but they don't relate to the uglier or the older women or the people that aren't into that foolishness. So what they end up doing is splitting and dividing the women, creating jealousy and also suspicion. But then send in a female organizer, who's *been* a clerk, who's not interested in screwing anybody, and it's an altogether different story.

Over the last couple of years part of the women's liberation movement has been these women's groups, inside companies, that are fighting to achieve better wages and working conditions and upward mobility for a few women. It's my point of view that these groups, while very important, will never take the women as far as union organizing will. First of all, there is no such thing as a union contract with a women's group. You don't have the backing of the rest of the labor movement. You are much too isolated from the support that you need. Secondly, the women who tend to be leaders of these groups very often tend to be promoted into management. So when the leaders are promoted, the gains that they have won often disappear.

II. BUILDING AN ORGANIZATION

As Margaret from the credit-card-company drive said, office workers don't want to "pull a fast one," get people signed up with an organization just on paper, and let someone else take control. Most office workers who start organizing feel, as Margaret did, that "What we wanted to do was organize the workers, *consciously* organize the workers so they can actually struggle together."

Margaret's group was insistent on controlling its own organizing campaign because it realized that the best way to make sure an organization would be democratic was to build it that way from the beginning. Traditional union organizers concentrate on getting people to sign up individually with the union, rather than building a strong group among themselves. Then later on, when members stay away from union meetings and expect the union staff to take care of everything, staffers complain about members' "apathy." But it was the organizers in the first place who gave people the impression that "the union" was a bunch of men in an office somewhere, not an organization of the workers themselves.

Leslie Sullivan talks about how her group tried to build a different kind of organization while she was working at Harvard Medical School. Carol discusses leadership in an organizing campaign, on the basis of her experience at a state university and in a recent industrial union drive. Claudia Roberson describes how she, as an organizer for the American Federation of State, County, and Municipal Employees, is able to help clerical workers organize themselves in Illinois State office buildings.

Leslie Sullivan: Margie Albert came and talked to us and said that we would have to have a large, strong core committee that was responsible and committed. We went around to all our friends and really pushed them to be on the committee. We explained to them that that meant a commitment to show up at the meetings, and to go out and talk to people about unions. We had to learn how to really function together *as a group*. We had to establish rules for our committee. We had to have a lot of respect for the other people on the committee, and for the committee itself, so we would respect its decisions. We made all the decisions ourselves, and we were all very concerned about each other and the group.

We started leafletting every week. We went public. We took men on. Whenever we put out a leaflet, all our names were on it, which I think is a very important point in that it inspired confidence. We started having meetings once a week, then twice a week, and eventually three times a week.

People became interested and called us for information. We'd call a meeting of a department to listen to one of us speak, then we'd encourage them to set up these meetings on a weekly basis. So we had about seven or eight different groups of about ten people. We called them satellite groups, and one of the people on the core committee would be responsible to see that they got together every week. This was a good way to spread information about the union. This was only for a period of a couple of months.

After that we started our card-signing. And from card-signing we've now developed building meetings, with people who are actually members. The responsibility of the members is to reach other people in their department, and to make sure that information gets passed on. We now have a very efficient newsletter system. In one morning, everybody in the medical area will receive a newsletter.

If you want people to take responsibility for negotiations and for running their own union, you really have to start *before* you have the union. We're trying to transfer the responsibility for the campaign from the organizing committee to the membership. The membership now meets every three weeks and all major policy decisions now are made by the membership.

Carol: At the university there was no single individual identified as the leader. The organizing committee was identified as a committee, which is important because, by making people aware of the committee, you convince them of the possibility of a group working in unison — that it's possible for them to function together. In the most recent organizing campaign I was involved with, this was done very consciously, with the insistence of the organizing committee. No meeting was ever run by the person that had run the previous meeting. Everybody had a chance at running a meeting and talking. It wasn't easy for some people to do that, but they felt that they were with friends, so they were encouraged. Some people chose to co-chair a meeting, so it worked out nicely.

The other important aspect of the university campaign was that we never had a union organizer identifiable by anybody on the campus, and that worked to our decided advantage. I strongly recommend that to people. Depending on a business agent starts, I think, by depending on a union organizer during the campaign.

Claudia Roberson: We try to get core groups in each office where they have more than fifteen or twenty clericals.

We start out by going in at lunch time and sitting down and talking with people about their grievances. I said, "OK, why don't we try to put all this into a questionnaire?"

The questionnaire asks people how much they make, what expenses they have, what they think they ought to make, just stuff like that. Then there's a multiple choice part with questions like, "My office is so roomy and ventilated and well lit." And you can answer "Always," "Sometimes," "Never," or "If it wasn't so dark and cold in here I could think more about this question." And "My office allows me to go and have training while I'm on state time so I can be upgraded." And the answers are "Always," "Sometimes," "Seldom," and "Upgrading is a new brand of typewriter."

When the answers to the questionnaire come in, we compile them so when the time comes to have contract demands we have a good start. But we will also go back and have them elect a negotiating committee. By that time they know each other and they can know who they might want to see representing them in a contract negotiation.

So it just starts from that little sitting around talking with five or six, and you grow to twelve, you grow to eighteen, and pretty soon you've got people involved that maybe never even talked before, because they considered themselves so insignificant behind that typewriter that nobody really wanted to know them.

III. GOING IN TO PERSONNEL

Management will try to give employee groups the impression that nothing *they* could possibly do would have any effect on management. Karen Nussbaum describes how they try to do this, and how to see through it.

Karen Nussbaum: If you build a group and then confront, say, a university administration, they will undoubtedly respond by saying something like, "Well, we're *very* happy that you brought your concerns to us. We will certainly take it under consideration. I *hope* you feel that our door is *always* open and that you'll come by again. That's what we're here for, and I thank you very much for coming here today."

After having worked to get a group of people together, to write up the grievances, and then to actually confront the guy — you don't know what to do when he just says, "Well, thank you very much." You feel like you've just done everything you possibly could, and all he has to do is sit on it. And they sit on it and sit on it, and then they'll say, "Well, you know, we *will* be having a personnel book coming out *very* soon that will answer a lot of these questions," or "Well, you know, we are about to hire somebody to act as a liaison person with the staff, because we believe there does need to be improved communications."

But what's *really* happening is that the guy is *shaking*. What if these people move on to the next step? He's just *banking* on being able to put them off, and usually he succeeds. What people don't understand is that the very *act* of asking for something is a threat. People don't realize the potential of that threat. The administration is calculating whether it's going to cost more for it *not* to give in than to give in. If unrest continues, and if unrest develops to the point when it impedes work — when it makes it difficult for personnel to do anything but deal with complaints, or when workers don't produce what they're supposed to, or when the threat of further organization, maybe union organization, becomes more real — then he's going to give in. People have to understand that managements aren't just a monolithic, powerful force that can grant privileges, but that there's a lot going on inside those closed doors. And employees have the power to affect that in several ways.

If personnel says, "Well, yes, we're working on it," then you *make* them work on it. You make them work their *asses* off on it. File forty complaints. Have everybody call up personnel to protest. If the issue is that you don't have a good grievance procedure, then over the next

three weeks, everybody should call up with a grievance
and say, "Well, you know, I'm having this problem and
I really don't know where to go, so I thought I'd call you
for help." You *bug* them with it. Or if the question is
benefits, then call them every day and say, "I don't understand my health benefits. Could you explain them to me?"
That's one way to make your power felt. You have the
power to disrupt. If you understand where your source
of power lies, you can be very imaginative about how
to use it to back up your demands.

The threat of legal action is another source of power.
Another is the possibility of forming a union. The reason
managements are so uptight about unions is that unions
give you the most power — the threat of going on strike.
Because, when you come right down to it, management
is dependent on employees to keep the place running.
Going on strike is the ultimate weapon of employees.

Here's an example of the way management tries to bluff
people. Some women from an insurance company came
to "9 to 5" with some issues that they had been stewing
about for a long time. One was a day off with pay that
they had been promised. The men in the company
had been invited out to the president's country club, and
got to take their families. The women were not only *not*
invited, but they weren't even getting the day off. The
whole summer was going by and they still hadn't gotten a
day off. And they had been *promised* a day off. There
were also other issues: they had dress codes; they weren't
allowed to smoke at their desks, but the men were.

We advised them to write up a petition about the day
off. They wrote up the petition, and within days one of
the managers got ahold of it, picked it up, and said,
"Girls, do you know what we do with these petitions? We
throw them right in the trash. I'm afraid it won't have
any impact. None whatsoever." They were completely
demoralized because they believed him. One week later a
memo came out saying that the day off with pay was
granted, women no longer had to wear skirts, and they
could also smoke at their desks. They're just *lying* when
they say they ignore things. They don't ignore a *thing*.

IV. BUT WHAT IF I GET FIRED?

Many of these descriptions are from people organizing on university campuses or in public office buildings. In those situations it's usually possible to be a little more open about what a group is doing. In banks, insurance companies, and other businesses, the atmosphere is usually more intimidating, and a person's first question is likely to be, "What if I get fired?"

This is not to say people are totally free to organize in universities and government offices (even though it *is* a legal right in all workplaces). People in those settings *have* gotten fired for organizing, too. Federal and state agencies are supposed to protect people from being fired for organizing. It's illegal to fire a person for trying to organize a union *or* for just getting together with other employees to try to change working conditions. It is also specifically illegal for people to be fired because they have protested against discrimination. But as we have seen, retaliation from the employer is still a real danger when employees organize. In spite of that, there *are* ways to guard against it, and to cut your losses.

Day Creamer: From the very first, when your group starts to meet, you keep very careful records of the fact that you are meeting. And if it looks like the employer is going to retaliate in some fashion, try to get him to do it where there are witnesses around. Try to get to him enough so that he will come right out and say that he's firing you because you're a troublemaker in the office. And then you go and file with the National Labor Relations Board. The NLRB can be helpful in terms of getting your job back and in getting you back wages, if you can't find a job in the meantime. But it's not one-hundred-percent sure. And there are some people, like legal secretaries, who are not covered by the NLRB. But the main thing I tell people is not to go off and do something stupid.

For example, do not tell your boss that you're a member of Women Employed. Do not tell your office manager that you are planning to get together the secretaries to talk about *x*, *y*, or *z*. People tend to do that. Don't do it.

You don't come in fifteen minutes late to work, giving him an excuse to fire you. You don't come in ten minutes late from lunch, giving him an excuse to fire you. You are super-nice to all of your bosses no matter how much they get under your skin. You are the model employee in all of those ways, making it much more difficult for them to get rid of you.

The second thing is that, yes, there is some risk. And yes, you might get fired. And that's just a reality of the kind of work we're talking about. Nobody said that it was going to be easy. Nobody ever said that we were going to win the battle without some people getting fired.

Julie (organizer, City Women for Action): There were things, after I filed my complaint, that were considered harassment. If a boss came in who normally said "Good morning" to you and he stopped saying "Good morning," that would be harassment. One boss not only stopped saying "Good morning" to me, but took the keys to the confidential file away from me, had my desk moved, and monitored my telephone calls. He gave me no work. I sat there for two months without a piece of work to do. So as I just sat there, I got madder and madder and filed more complaints.

My advice to someone who's being subjected to this kind of thing is: Don't take it personally. It's not directed personally at you. It's just in their heads and they can't deal with it. They haven't grown, their minds haven't grown, they're living in the Dark Ages. You just can't talk to them so you should just forget about trying to change them. They themselves are not important. Changing the *system* is important.

Karen Nussbaum: People *do* have legal rights to organize, in unions or in committees or whatever, and they ought to exercise them. A lot of times just the fear of legal action is enough to make employers shape up. All these suits cost them a lot of money in the courts. It's important to use whatever legal sanctions you do have. But there's still a risk. In order to organize, people just have to make the decision that it's worth the risk, when it's no longer worth it to work under those conditions.

V. A FINAL NOTE

Maxine Jenkins: You can start out with two people and grow to five, but as long as you're tenacious and you do your homework and you're not afraid and you can accept defeats as they come along, you'll win!

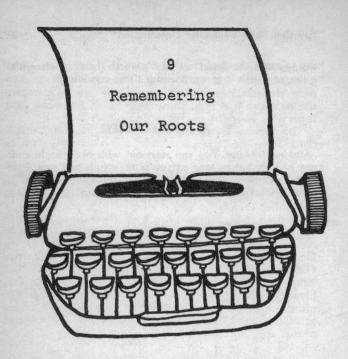

9

Remembering

Our Roots

This is not the only time in American history that office workers have organized. The roots of the movement go back to the second decade of this century, when clericals were joining unions and demanding better treatment on the job. By that time, a union movement had been growing for nearly a hundred years, fighting for such basic things as the eight-hour day and the right to organize at all. At the same time, a movement for women's rights was demanding legal equality and greater job opportunities.

Telephone operators were among the first women clerical workers to join unions. An expert's study in 1915 "proved" that they were impossible to organize: they were too young, there was too much turnover and competition for jobs.[1] Not having read the report, telephone operators joined the International Brotherhood [*sic*] of Electrical Workers (IBEW), and the union soon established a Telephone Operators' Department. Within the union, the women were allowed to pay only half the dues — and given only half the voting power! Later, other phone company clericals joined the "independent" phone company unions which had been encouraged by management, since these were easier to control.

The next big organizing effort by office workers came in the 1930's. The Depression had sparked the biggest period of labor-organizing in the country's history. The new activity produced a new organization, The Congress of Industrial Organizations (CIO), which sought to open up the union movement to *all* workers, not just the elite few who had skilled trades.

Clericals who worked for the government organized within the CIO as part of the United Public Workers of America. Office workers in private industry joined the United Office and Professional Workers of America (UOPWA), also in the CIO. That union started in New York, but spread to other cities, with locals in insurance, banking, and publishing, as well as locals for groups like artists and social workers. The recollections of two former activists in the UOPWA describe what it was like to organize at that time:

JANE BENEDICT

Jane Benedict was active in a publishing employees' local of the UOPWA in the 1930's. She is now an organizer for a tenants' rights group in New York City. Recently, groups of young women who work for publishing companies have been dropping by her office to hear her stories of organizing, and to get a different angle on recent events.

When I first got involved in what eventually became the union in publishing, it was the Depression. This was a tremendously exciting period. This was the period in which there were sit-downs in auto, in steel — simply taking over a plant by sitting down. There was generally a growing militancy on the part of the labor movement. The CIO broke away from the AFL, which had been sitting on its rear end for years. The CIO was a very innovative, exciting, insurgent movement. To your generation it's almost impossible to imagine the AFL-CIO doing any of the things that the CIO did during that period. The CIO was a very exciting place to be.

I belonged to the Book and Magazine Guild, CIO. It was Local 18 of the United Office and Professional Workers of America. It organized a number of the publishing houses. Our first contracts were Knopf, Random House, and Viking, in the offices. Altogether we probably had twenty or thirty contracts in New York. Besides book publishing, we got into magazine and nonprofit organizations. We had some bookstores.

The union was an exciting union. It had lots of volunteers. An organization that is carrying on an insurgent battle cannot be run simply by a paid staff. That way, it becomes a bureaucracy. You have to have certain guidelines and approaches, otherwise you have chaos. But I do believe you've got to have as many people involved in the work as you can possibly find.

Women were well represented in the leadership of the union. I was, at one point, the executive secretary of the union. Later I became the president. We had two male full-time organizers and two or three women. It was pretty evenly divided. We had several paid office assistants. They were all women.

We raised the issue of discrimination against minorities. It was a very pioneering issue. It is difficult to imagine in this day and age. Black people in white-collar jobs were almost unheard of. There were a few victories, but they were few and far between. The women's issue wasn't raised too much. There was the struggle for promotions, but certainly not the conscious struggle that there is today.

The natural question is, well, after all, if you organized and you made headway in publishing, what happened? Why do we find no trace of your union? The answer is that the United Office and Professional Workers, which was the union of which we were a part, died. It went out of existence during the Joseph McCarthy period, as did a number of the unions that were the more insurgent in the CIO.

It's very difficult for you to imagine what the McCarthy period was like. It was a very bitter, to many people, an utterly frightening, period. Many people never became active in anything again. They were simply so terrified of losing jobs, of being smeared, that they didn't share their opinions with anybody. Frightening thing. Just stultifying. And in that atmosphere our union died. Anybody who had ever had any *gesture* of interest in *anything* was called a Communist. And people paid the penalty. And the union movement paid the penalty. That's what happened to our union. And I *do* think that's a lesson for this period, because we could have it again. One has to be aware of it, and be convinced that that kind of thing has to be stood up against.

FLORENCE LUSCOMB

Florence Luscomb's interest in women's rights began at the age of five, when her mother took her to hear Susan B. Anthony speak. When Florence was already in her fifties, she began organizing office workers with the UOPWA in Boston. Now in her late eighties, she occasionally speaks at "9 to 5" rallies and meetings, to encourage and inspire the current generation of office workers, and to share with them her experiences from the past.

I was an executive secretary when the CIO was organized. One of their branches was an office workers' organization, the United Office and Professional Workers. I attended its founding convention. Then I came back to Boston and started getting in touch with various of my friends to form a local union here. A year or two later I was chosen as the president.

We were never a large group. I don't think we were ever more than fifty. But we carried on an active campaign to try to get our organization into various offices that did employ a large number of office workers.

I remember one interesting experience. There was a large business firm which had something like fifty office workers. They were paid unspeakably low wages, and had terrifically poor working conditions. Long hours and all that. One of the members in our local happened to get acquainted with one of the girls who worked in this firm. She told us about it and thought we might be able to organize there.

She gave us the names of many of the workers. We visited them in their homes, and we built up quite an interest in joining the union. We had quite a sizeable group, and they were talking to the other workers, so we felt that we would really have this large office organized, and be able to call a strike if necessary.

The management got wind of this movement among their workers, and they proceeded immediately to raise their wages and better some of their conditions. The minute they did that, none of the girls were interested in the union any longer. That was a typical experience. In a great many offices, we succeeded in getting better conditions and better pay just because the union existed. Their workers were getting interested in it and management felt that it would be faced with a unionized office if it didn't improve things. So although our own membership was never large, we did succeed in getting better conditions for the office workers in Boston.

There came along, in the late forties, the McCarthy era, when there was great red-baiting against organized labor. Some of our members *were* Communists. They did very devoted work for the union. Anybody who belonged to the Communist Party didn't belong to it unless they had a real conviction. But during this period of red-baiting, our union simply went out of existence.

·   ·   ·   ·   ·   ·   ·

The specific way McCarthyism attacked unions was through a law that said that all union officers had to swear they weren't Communists or any other type of "subversive." This requirement threw the whole union movement into confusion. Individuals and unions started fighting each other rather than the employers. Some people used anti-Communism as a vehicle to capture union offices. Some

unions were expelled from the CIO because they refused
to go along with the non-Communist pledge — including
the two major clerical unions, the UOPWA and the United
Public Workers.

In the early forties, a more conservative office workers'
union had been founded — the Office Employees International Union (now the OPEIU). The OEIU benefited from
this mess by picking up groups of employees from the
UOPWA, while assuring everybody that *they* certainly
weren't radical. In fact, their president said, they wanted
"amicable" relationships with employers.[2] Nothing for the
boss to worry about.

When the dust settled, the United Public Workers and
the United Office and Professional Workers were destroyed.
The OEIU continued limping along as a small, conservative union. A new public employees' union, the American Federation of State, County, and Municipal Employees, was formed, but grew slowly in the beginning.
Meanwhile, anyone suspected of being interested in any
type of social change was branded a Communist. People
were brought before congressional investigating committees
— the most famous one led by Senator Joe McCarthy. For
many people, investigation meant losing jobs. The threat
of investigation drove some people to suicide. Known
Communist leaders were thrown in jail under a law called
the Smith Act. The "silent generation" of the 1950's came
into being. After terrorizing anyone who protested, political leaders complained that the public was "apathetic." It
was a *silenced* generation.

But meanwhile, the clerical work force was growing rapidly. As the sixties began, the country started to emerge
from its political paranoia as the civil rights and peace
movements started a new process of questioning. Union
activity also picked up. Public-employee unions, with many
clerical members, mushroomed during the sixties. In the
private sector, every year more groups of white-collar
workers joined unions. Then, in the late sixties, a new
movement for women's rights made itself a powerful force
in American life. At first the activists were mainly professional women and college students, but as the movement

grew, it created a new awareness among millions of women. Because of sex discrimination, many of these women worked in "job ghettos," including clerical occupations. Awareness led to anger. Anger led to protest. A new movement of office workers was born.

10

"It's an Exciting Time!"

The office workers' movement has brought about many changes in the lives of its participants. These changes are significant, not only for the people involved, but for everyone who is part of the large and expanding clerical workforce. And as this movement grows, it will have an impact on the women's movement, on unions, and on American life.

Even in its beginning stages, the movement of office workers has been able to win more money, more job security, maternity leaves, better benefits, and fairer promotion systems for many people. These victories are part of a larger struggle to stop employers from using women as a low-paid, docile pool of labor. Clerical employers traditionally have felt free to offer women low pay and poor conditions, because of the job ghetto — they knew women couldn't do better anywhere else. As some working women begin to win improvements, it becomes harder for *all* employers to get away with poor treatment of women workers. New alternatives are created and standards are raised. The office is a crucial place to carry on this struggle because so much of the female workforce is clerical — one third of all women workers.

But the women involved in this movement have created a second, equally important change — the change in themselves. The secretaries, clerks, typists, and bank tellers who speak in this book have all had to struggle with their own fears, self-doubts, and lack of knowledge. They have had to fight against their own and other people's stereotypes just as hard as they have had to fight against their employers. And the victories in that fight have been dramatic:

Day Creamer: It's helping women to be able to speak in public. To be able to confront someone and to make demands on the person. To be able to negotiate with that person and not feel intimidated. To feel confident in your position, in knowing that you're right, and in having the information. Being able to think about questions of strategy and how we move to achieve the things we want. How do you chair a meeting? How do you work in a committee?

One woman who's in the organization said, "I learned that I had some rights. And I learned that I could be assertive on my job and understand when my rights were being infringed — and that I didn't have to take it. And I learned how I could approach dealing with that without coming across totally obnoxious. But understanding who I am as a person — that made me feel really good about myself."

Maxine Jenkins: After the committees are built, newsletters have been published, and clerical workers have come together around a common cause, they hold up their heads very high. They are very proud. It's a visible change that you can see in the offices, in the way they conduct themselves. It's like, we don't have to be ashamed to be clerks anymore. That change just begins to shine all over their faces.

.   .   .   .

Like the salary increases, this personal change is part of a larger process — women freeing themselves from a subordinate place in society. The stereotypes of clerical workers — stupid, frivolous, weak, useful only to help men do the *real* work — are just stereotypes of all women, translated into an office setting.

The office workers' movement, in challenging and disproving these stereotypes, has a special meaning for the women's movement. Most of the early women's movement, especially the most publicized part, was made up of professionals, students, and upper-middle-class housewives. While challenging stereotypes of women, some of *these* people also thought that secretaries were stupid and unimportant. Many women office workers have stories to tell about the contemptuous attitudes and bad treatment they received from women at higher levels, some of whom considered themselves part of the women's movement or even belonged to the same women's rights group as the clerical workers did.

It's possible to convince someone that a woman lawyer or college professor is a serious, intelligent person. But many people see those women as exceptions — they're not "just" secretaries or waitresses or housewives, like most women. So when clerical workers begin to organize and assert themselves, it is a much more basic challenge to stereotypes of women, and very important to *all* women who want real change.

This movement also challenges the idea that the purpose of a women's movement is to clear the way so that individual women can compete with men to become bank presidents or astronauts. Only a few people of either sex ever get to the top — and those who do are usually the ones with other advantages, like being born there to start with, and being white. Even if half those top positions were filled by females, it would still leave most women, like most men, doing ordinary jobs. If that were the only change, women would still be getting paid less, treated worse, and looked down upon.

"Womanpower," says a TV ad, "it's too good to waste." And the picture shows a typing pool. *Waste?* Clerical workers play an important role in keeping the country going, many doing difficult and skilled work. The ad implies that if a person is still in the typing pool, she's no good, or useless. "Liberated" women are all supposedly rising above being "mere" clerical workers.

A movement of office workers challenges this idea. It seeks to improve the situation of a whole group of women through collective action. One of those improvements is a fair promotion system. But others are important too: decent pay, better conditions, and respect for office workers as people and as workers.

The office workers' movement emphasizes winning better conditions for women as a *group*. This emphasis has led office workers to support the efforts of other working women pushing for better treatment. Office workers in Union WAGE have participated in the campaign for laws giving more rights to household workers. The "9 to 5" newsletter publicizes and supports the Boston restaurant workers' union. Women Employed campaigned for the rights of janitoresses in a Chicago bank. The message is that a movement for women's rights has to benefit ordinary women, not just help a few get to the top.

The movement of office workers also has a message for unions. Office workers want to control their own organizations, and demand that groups representing them take women and women's needs seriously. Because so few office workers are now organized, they have a chance to build new kinds of organizations in which rank-and-file control and the leadership of women are taken seriously. These organizations in turn can provide inspiration and models for other groups of working women, inside and outside unions.

And to the corporations that employ them, office workers are saying that they demand some power over the decisions that affect them, and will not allow themselves to be used in just any way the company happens to find convenient or profitable. This message also contributes to something larger — the efforts of American workers to win self-determination, against the rule of corporations.

Day Creamer: Probably the overall general message is that working women have rights. It's also understanding that, really and truly, the long range changes are going to depend on collective effort. Even though some of us will be able to fight and claw and scratch and make it somewhere individually, *most* of us are not going to be able to do that because of the nature of the corporate structure, because of sex discrimination, and because the corporation's first and primary interest is in how much money they're going to make. Our interests as employees are going to be secondary. And it's only when we understand that we have to organize ourselves together that we're going to be able to even approach dealing with that whole question of what's more important — the profits the company can make, or the situation of the employees?

How do we win? We don't win by people sitting down and being nice to each other across the table. We win by how much power we've got and how much they've got, and what we can do to them if they don't agree to what we want. And learning that lesson — that sense of power — it's just incredible what it does to women's concept of themselves and their concept of social change. That's what we are talking about — this whole sense of the arrogance of corporate power. The arrogance of a system that's only concerned about profits.

It's my feeling that the movement of working women has potential for being a very potent social force in American society in the next ten years, say. Working women are getting angrier and angrier on all levels, whether it's wages or benefits or the lack of respect on the job or options for promotions — whatever those things are, the anger is growing and building. And that is going to stimulate organizing of one sort or another, whether it's union-organizing or whether it's these in-office committee kinds of things.

I think it can potentially feed into a lot of the other sort of populist, citizen-movement, grass-roots kinds of things that are developing all over the country. And potentially there is going to come a time when a coalition of these various groupings is going to be possible. The potential is incredible. Working women haven't yet been recognized for the force that they are. It's an exciting time!

          ·   ·   ·   ·   ·   ·   ·

The power and potential of a movement ultimately rest on its personal meaning for the people involved, and the changes it can make in their lives. Two Women Employed members describe what the movement has meant to them:

Harriet Wessling: I think it's had a good effect. I'm not nearly as dependent on other people as I used to be, and I feel now that I'm not a dummy. You can get that opinion of yourself just working day in and day out when people say, "Oh, you're only a secretary." By being in Women Employed, I got to talk to many other women who have the same feelings, and I finally came to realize that it's not *me*. There's nothing wrong with me. I'm a very competent person. It's *them*! It's the atmosphere *they* create. And I'm going to get them for it!

Kathy Bacom: It's really exciting to realize that the efforts I am making now will make a difference. I have five younger sisters. I would like them not to have to go through the kinds of things that I have. I'm twenty-nine years old, and there is a sense of failure — a sense of not having done anything, of what's wrong with me. But then when you realize that most other women are pretty much in the same boat, it makes you feel a little better about it. I would like to make a difference, and I think it's probably oriented towards my little sisters. I would like them to have a break.

NOTES

2 OFFICE WORK

1. Harry Braverman, *Labor and Monopoly Capital* (New York and London: Monthly Review Press, 1974), p. 295.
2. C. Wright Mills, *White Collar* (New York: Oxford University Press, 1953), p. 189.
3. Bureau of Labor Statistics, *Handbook of Labor Statistics, 1974,* Bulletin #1825, Washington, D.C., p. 74.
4. Braverman, *loc. cit.*
5. Jan Manette, *The Working Girl in a Man's World* (New York: Hawthorn Books, 1966), p. 54.
6. Research Director Mr. Reedy, Office and Professional Employees International Union, in an interview, December 11, 1974.
7. James Culliton, Assistant to the Vice-President for Administration and Personnel, MIT, in *The Tech,* March 12, 1974.
8. In an interview, December 20, 1974.
9. IBM's *Word Processing* magazine, January/February, 1974.
10. C. L. Littlefield, R. M. Rachel, and D. L. Caruth, *Office and Administrative Management* (Englewood Cliffs, N.J.: Prentice-Hall, 1970), p. 428.
11. Braverman, *op. cit.,* pp. 296–7.
12. Paul Flaim and Nick Peters, "Usual Gross Earnings of American Workers," *Monthly Labor Review,* March, 1972.
13. Bureau of Labor Statistics, *Autumn 1974 Urban Family Budgets,* p. 1, and *National Survey of Professional Administrative, Technical and Clerical Pay,* March, 1973, Bulletin 1804, p. 14.
14. Flaim and Peters, *op. cit.,* p. 250.
15. *The Real Paper,* February 20, 1974.

16. *Union WAGE,* July/August, 1972.

17. *Nine to Five,* June/July, 1974.

18. *New York Times,* August 8, 1974.

19. *Guardian,* April 16, 1975.

20. Littlefield et al., *op. cit.,* p. 250.

21. Bureau of Labor Statistics, *Technological Trends in Major American Industries,* Bulletin #1474, Washington, D.C., 1966; sections on banking and insurance, *passim.*

22. Bureau of Labor Statistics, *Technological Trends,* p. 253.

23. Ida R. Hoos, "When the Computer Takes Over the Office," *Harvard Business Review,* July/August, 1960.

24. *Wall Street Journal,* October 17, 1974.

25. *Word Processing,* January/February, 1974.

26. Georgina Smith, *Office Automation and White Collar Employment,* Institute of Management and Labor Relations, Rutgers University, Bulletin #6, 1960.

27. Bureau of Labor Statistics, *Technological Trends,* p. 247.

28. Audrey Freedman and Edgar Weinberg, "Changing Manpower Needs in Telephone Offices," *Monthly Labor Review,* February, 1968.

29. *Union WAGE,* January/February, 1973.

30. Elizabeth Faulkner Baker, *Technology and Women's Work* (New York: Columbia University Press, 1964), p. 73.

31. Bureau of Labor Statistics, *1974 Handbook,* table 19, pl. 69–73.

32. Women's Bureau, Department of Labor, *Women Workers Today,* p. 5.

33. Margery Davies, "A Woman's Place is at the Typewriter," *Radical America,* September/October 1974, is the source for the discussion of why clerical work became women's work.

34. *Nine to Five* newsletter, April/May, 1974.

35. *Union WAGE,* January/February, 1973.

36. Nine to Five, *Claim Against the Boston Insurance Industry,* 1974.

37. Lorraine Eyde, "The Status of Women in State and Local Government," *Public Personnel Management,* May, 1973.

38. *Monthly Labor Review,* May, 1974.

39. Women's Bureau, *Women Workers Today,* p. 6.

40. Women's Bureau, "Fact Sheet on the Earnings Gap," December, 1971.

41. Bureau of the Census, *Statistical Abstract of the United States, 1973,* Washington, D.C., 1973, p. 245.

42. Bureau of Labor Statistics, "Industry Wage Survey: Banking," Bulletin #1466, 1964, p. 6, and "Industry Wage Survey: Life Insurance," Bulletin #1569, 1966, pp. 5–6.

43. Nine to Five, *Claim Against the Boston Insurance Industry.*

44. Baker, *op. cit.*, pp. 72–73.

45. *Ibid.*, p. 74.

46. Women's Bureau, "The Myth and the Reality," 1972.

47. *Monthly Labor Review,* May, 1974.

48. Women's Bureau, "The Myth and the Reality."

49. This analysis was taken partly from Stephen A. Marglin, "What Do Bosses Do?" in the *Review of Radical Political Economics,* Summer, 1974.

50. The summary of the "scientific management" procedures which follows is discussed from management's point of view in Littlefield et al., *op. cit.*; see, e.g., pp. 382, 133, 310, 314, and 402.

51. *Nine to Five* newsletter, April/May, 1973.

52. Littlefield et al., *op. cit.*, p. 352.

53. Nine to Five, *Claim Against the Boston Insurance Industry.*

54. Sar A. Levitan and William B. Johnston, "Job Design, Reform, Enrichment — Exploring the Limits," *Monthly Labor Review,* July, 1973.

3 ORIGINS OF THE CURRENT MOVEMENT

1. See, for instance, Industrial Relations Counselors, Inc., *White Collar Restiveness: A Growing Challenge,* Industrial Relations Monograph #22, 1963.

2. *Harvard Business Review,* March/April, 1971.

3. Margie Albert, "Something New in the Women's Movement," *New York Times,* October 28, 1973.

7 UP AGAINST MAHOGANY ROW

1. Industrial Relations Counselors, Inc., *White Collar Restiveness: A Growing Challenge.* Industrial Relations Monograph #22, 1963.

2. Prentice-Hall, *Personal Memorandum — How to Meet the Problem of White Collar Organizing,* New York, 1955.

3. Bureau of Labor Statistics, "Employee Compensation in

the Private Non-farm Economy, 1966," Bulletin # 1627, 1969.

4. Stated at a seminar, "How to Maintain Non-Union Status," sponsored by the American Association of Industrial Management, New England and the Associated Industries of Massachusetts, in Newton, Mass., February 5, 1975.

5. Bureau of National Affairs, *White Collar Report*, September 21, 1973.

6. *Wall Street Journal*, November 14, 1974.

7. C. L. Littlefield, F. M. Rachel, and D. L. Caruth, *Office and Administrative Management* (Englewood Cliffs, N.J.: Prentice-Hall, 1970).

8. Grace Ann Dunphy in *Union WAGE*, January/February, 1975.

9. Stated at a workshop, "Management Education for Secretaries," Providence, R.I., November 6, 1974.

10. *Clerks' County*, Alameda County, California, January 11, 1973.

11. Littlefield, et al., *op. cit.*

12. Harold Kowal in an interview, January 25, 1975.

13. *Ibid.*

14. *White Collar Report*, January 12, 1973.

15. National Industrial Conference Board, *White Collar Unionization*, Studies in Personnel Policy, #220, New York, 1970.

16. Lynn Karsten, former union organizer, interview, December 3, 1974.

17. Yale University, *Union Organizing Drive Manual* (mimeographed pamphlet for supervisors), 1971.

18. Industrial Relations Counselors, Inc., *op. cit.*

19. Prentice-Hall, *Personal Memorandum.*

20. Kowal, *op. cit.*

21. John McKeon, OPEIU organizer, interview, December 10, 1974.

22. *White Collar Report*, September 21, 1973.

23. National Industrial Conference Board, *op. cit.*

24. From the seminar, "How to Maintain Non-Union Status," *op. cit.*

9   REMEMBERING OUR ROOTS

1. Elizabeth Faulkner Baker, *Technology and Women's Work* (New York: Columbia University Press, 1964).

2. *Ibid.*, p. 362.

I. GLOSSARY

Affirmative Action: a term used by the federal government in setting regulations for those companies it contracts with. It means that any organization that is given a government contract can't discriminate against women or minorities. The company is also required to take positive steps to make up for the effects of *past* discrimination, such as making extra efforts to hire and promote women and minorities.

Business Agent: a full-time, paid representative of a local union whose job is to help enforce the contract and represent employees.

Captive Audience Meetings: a union term for meetings of workers called by management, on company time and property. The purpose of these meetings is to try to persuade workers to vote against union representation, and they usually take place during a union organizing drive.

Collective Bargaining: a process through which employees, through their representatives, deal with their employer *as a group* to set salaries and conditions, rather than each person trying to get the best deal she/he can by talking to the boss alone. It's the basic idea of union, but it doesn't have to be done through an established union.

Goals and Timetables: a shorthand term for the strictest kind of affirmative action. It means the company has to promise that a certain percentage of the people at each job level will be women and minorities (goals) by a given date (timetables).

International: a term commonly used as part of the names of unions because they have locals in Canada and the United States.

Master Contract: a union contract covering several companies in one industry.

Protective Laws: State laws passed near the turn of the century, regulating conditions of work for women. The laws usually set standards for things like rest breaks and facilities, and limit the hours of work. The laws have helped men as well as women by regulating working conditions. But they have also been used as an excuse to pay women less and exclude them from many jobs.

Servicing: the day-to-day enforcement of a union contract by a business agent.

Steward or *Shop Steward:* an employee who, under a union contract, officially represents other employees on the job, enforcing the contract and helping people with grievances.

Trusteeship or *Receivership:* direct control of a local union's affairs by the international officers. Most unions have some provision for the international to put a local in trusteeship when it is judged to be incapable of running itself. Although the formal charges are usually matters like election fraud or financial mismanagement, it can be a way of suppressing new leadership within a union.

Union Election: a vote of all the employees to decide whether they want a particular organization to represent them in collective bargaining. If a majority votes "yes," the employer must negotiate with that organization.

II. GOVERNMENT AGENCIES
THAT PROTECT YOUR JOB RIGHTS

(*Warning:* These descriptions are very brief and leave out many procedures, exceptions, etc. If you need the protection of any of these agencies, check the phone book for the office nearest you, and contact the agency for more detailed information.)

Equal Employment Opportunity Commission. This is a federal agency which enforces Title VII of the 1964 Civil Rights Act. That act outlaws job discrimination based on sex, race, color, religion, or national origin. It includes discrimination in hiring, firing, pay, conditions, or privileges. If the EEOC investigation finds discrimination, it usually tries to arrange an agreement between employer and employees. If no agreement is reached, the EEOC decides whether to take the employer to court, or leave it up to the individual to sue the employer.

State or City Anti-Discrimination Agencies exist in many areas and protect the same rights as the EEOC.

Wage and Hour Division, Department of Labor, enforces only one thing: equal pay for equal work. It covers cases where a man and a woman do similar work and get paid different amounts. The work does not have to be *exactly* the same, however, and the job *titles* don't have to be the same. The agency can sue the employer, or leave it up to the individual.

Office of Federal Contract Compliance enforces the anti-discrimination requirements for federal contractors, including affirmative action. If an investigation shows a company is violating the requirements, the agency can order a hearing. Theoretically, the government revokes contracts of companies that discriminate or fail to provide good affirmative action plans. In practice this is hardly ever done.

National Labor Relations Board enforces the National Labor Relations Act, which says that employees have the right to join together to bargain collectively with employers. It's illegal for employers to try in any way to stop them, including threats, punishments, firings, bribes, promises, intimidation. The law protects not only union organizing, but any "concerted action" by employees to improve wages, conditions, etc. It also establishes a procedure for union elections, and says that if a union wins the election, the employer must bargain with that union in good faith. If you are organizing a union, you should call your local NLRB office and ask for more details. If you think your employer is breaking the law, call the NLRB. The board has the power to order the employer to stop, or to remedy his actions with reinstatement or back pay. Two pamphlets explaining NLRB rights and procedures can be ordered from the NLRB, 1717 Pennsylvania Ave NW, Washington, D.C. 20570: "A Layman's Guide to Basic Law Under the NLRB" and "Your Government Conducts an Election."

III. UNIONS

Some of the unions organizing clerical workers are: Service Employees International Union; Office and Professional Employees International Union; Distributive Workers of America; American Federation of State, County, and Municipal Employees; Communications Workers of America; International Brotherhood of Electrical Workers; American Federation of Government Employees; United Auto Workers; United Steel Workers of America; and the Teamsters.

The Coalition of Labor Union Women is a national organization of women in unions, which was established in 1974. It can be contacted through 8000 E. Jefferson, Detroit, Michigan.

All of these organizations vary from place to place. Locals differ from each other, even within the same union. In addition, the internationals differ from each other in approach, commitment to organizing, and amount of democracy. Before affiliating with any union, you should check it out nationally *and* locally. Get copies of the union constitution and copies of recent contracts the union has negotiated in your area. Talk with union representatives and try to find out how they feel about local autonomy, democracy, and fighting discrimination. Find out what disciplinary actions have been taken against locals, and the full stories behind these actions. *Most important,* talk with other people who are represented by the union in your area and see how they feel about it. If some people in your company are already unionized, talk with them about their union. It may be to your advantage to belong to the same one, or at least to cooperate with it, for more strength.

IV. WOMEN'S ORGANIZATIONS
AND PUBLICATIONS

Women's Action Alliance, 370 Lexington Ave., New York, New York 10017, publishes a packet called "Sex Discrimination in State and Local Governments," but much of the information would also be helpful to women in private employment. The packet consists of the following pamphlets: "How to Tell When You're Being Discriminated Against on the Basis of Sex," "Patterns of Sex Discrimination in

State and Local Governments," "How to Document Sex Discrimination," "Legal Remedies," "Affirmative Action," and "Organizing Women Employees."

The Municipal Women's Project, 140 Clarendon St., Boston, Mass., publishes two pamphlets: "Sex Discrimination, How Do You Know When It's Happening to You?" and "Laws that Protect Women on the Job."

Union WAGE, P.O. Box 462, Berkeley, Cal. 94701: publishes a bimonthly newspaper for working women and a pamphlet series including: "Working Women and Their Organizations: 150 Years of Struggle," "Women in the Labor Movement," "Labor Heroines: Ten Women who Led the Struggle," and a new pamphlet on how to organize within an established union.

Women Employed, 37 S. Wabash, Chicago, Ill., and

9 to 5, 140 Clarendon St., Boston, Mass., each publishes a newsletter and occasional research reports.

Women Office Workers, 600 Lexington Avenue, Room 508, New York, New York 10022, an action and research organization for women office workers.

Cleveland Women Working, 9721 Harnder Ave., Cleveland, Ohio 44102, organizing information and publications about working women in Cleveland.

Women's Action Training Center, 1941 High St., Oakland, Cal., publishes a pamphlet called *Growing Older Female,* containing information, discussion, and a list of resources for older women.

NOW Committee on Women in Office Work, 1957 E. 73rd St. Chicago, Ill., publishes a booklet on actions office workers can take to improve their job situation.

Federally Employed Women (contact through your local Women's Bureau office) publishes a newsletter and reports on the status of women in the federal government.

V. TRAINING

The Midwest Academy, 600 Fullerton, Chicago, Ill., offers courses on organizing skills to groups who can send a member to Chicago. They also will go to other locations to give classes.

VI. BOOKS

Baker, Elizabeth Faulkner, *Technology and Women's Work*
     (New York: Columbia University Press, 1964). Good
     summary of the history of women's work, including offices
     in general and the phone company in particular. Includes
     a chapter briefly summarizing the history of clerical union-
     ism.

Benet, Mary Kathleen, *The Secretarial Ghetto* (New York:
     McGraw-Hill, 1973). Offers a personal, historical, and psy-
     chological view of office work and office roles.

Braverman, Harry, *Labor and Monopoly Capital: The Degra-
     dation of Work in the Twentieth Century* (New York:
     Monthly Review Press, 1974). Includes an excellent chap-
     ter on clerical work, giving an historical and economic
     analysis of how office work is changing. Also includes a
     chapter on scientific management. These chapters are in-
     dispensable to an understanding of the modern office.

Bureau of Labor Statistics, Bulletin #1474, *Technological
     Trends in Major American Industries*, 1966. Helpful sum-
     maries of automation and its effect on employment, includ-
     ing clerical occupations.

Mills, C. Wright, *White Collar* (New York: Oxford University
     Press, 1951). A classic sociological and cultural descrip-
     tion of white-collar work, including a chapter on clerical
     work and a discussion of white-collar unions.

Sturmthal, A., ed., *White Collar Trade Unions* (Urbana, Illi-
     nois: University of Illinois Press, 1966). A collection of
     articles about white-collar unions in many countries in-
     cluding the United States.

VII. ARTICLES

Davies, Margery, "A Woman's Place is at the Typewriter,"
     Radical America, September/October, 1974. An historical
     account of how and why office work became women's work.

Davis, Susan, "Organizing from Within," *Ms*, August, 1972.
     Discusses women's caucuses in the workplace.

Eyde, Lorraine D., "Status of Women in State and Local Gov-
     ernment," *Public Personnel Management*, May, 1973. A
     statistical analysis.

Hoos, Ida, "When the Computer Takes Over the Office," *Harvard Business Review,* July/August, 1960.

Monthly Labor Review, "Usual Weekly Earnings of American Workers," March, 1972. Breaks down statistics by sex, race, and occupation.

Monthly Labor Review, May, 1974, special issue on "Women in the Workplace."

VIII. STATISTICS

The best source of statistics is the federal Department of Labor, especially the Bureau of Labor Statistics and the Women-en's Bureau. Their publications are available in many libraries, or by writing to them in Washington. Even if you have never used statistical publications, you can use these, with a little practice. Two tips: 1) Consult the reference librarian. She/he knows how to use them and it's her/his job to help you. 2) Read the titles and headings on charts carefully and think about what they mean.

A few of the most widely used publications are:

Bureau of Labor Statistics: *Monthly Labor Review* (magazine); *Handbook of Labor Statistics* (yearly publication); *National Survey of Professional, Administrative, Technical and Clerical Pay* (yearly); *Area Wage Surveys* (for particular geographical areas); *Industry Wage Surveys.*

Women's Bureau: *The Myth and the Reality* (1972), *Women in Labor Unions* (1974), *Women Workers Today* (1971), *Background Facts on Women Workers in the United States* (1970).

Census Bureau (Department of Commerce): *Statistical Abstract of the United States* (yearly).

IX. INFORMATION FROM
MAHOGANY ROW

Bureau of National Affairs, *White Collar Report* (available from BNA, 1231 25th St., NW, Washington, D.C. 20037).

Comprehensive weekly report on organizing and all other information about white-collar workers. The catch is that it's too expensive for an individual or small group to afford, but unions could order it.

National Industrial Conference Board, *White Collar Unionization.* Personnel Policy study #220, New York, 1970. Detailed report on recent trends and survey of white-collar union campaigns.

Two older pamphlets are interesting because they offer insight into management thinking: Industrial Relations Counselors, Inc., "White Collar Restiveness: A Growing Challenge," Industrial Relations Monograph #22, 1963, and from Prentice-Hall, "Personal Memorandum: How to Meet the Problems of White Collar Organizing," New York, 1955.